Critical Incident Management

An On-Scene Guide for Law Enforcement Supervisors

D1291872

Critical Incident Management

An On-Scene Guide for Law Enforcement Supervisors

Vincent F. Faggiano

Thomas T. Gillespie

K&M Publishers

Tulsa, Oklahoma

Important Note

Products and services provided by K&M Publishers, Inc. are intended for educational purposes only. K&M Publishers, Inc. makes no warranties or guarantees, either expressed or implied, as to the legal effect of the information supplied in those products and services. Further, K&M Publishers, Inc. assumes no liability associated with providing this information. You are encouraged to seek the advice of your own legal counsel or that of your sponsoring agency or entity regarding this material.

Credits

Development Editor: Jeffrey P. Gregory

Cover design: Brian England

Interior art: Brian England and Jane Kleinschmidt

Production services: Traci Pearson

Printed in the United States of America

10 9 8 7 6 5 4 3 2 1

ISBN 0-9727134-2-5

Dedication

The authors dedicate this book to all the brave police, fire, and EMS personnel who on a daily basis respond to critical incidents in the face of tremendous risks and danger. Without a doubt, we learn more from our students than our students ever learn from us.

Acknowledgements

The authors and the publisher wish to acknowledge the outstanding contribution made by **Jeffrey P. Gregory**, the Development Editor for this project. Jeff helped the authors organize their thoughts and say exactly what they wanted to say.

The authors and the publisher further wish to acknowledge and thank the reviewers of the manuscript for their time, effort, and insights that help make this a better book.

- **John W. Brenner**, Law Enforcement Loss Control Specialist, The Kentucky League of Cities, and Kentucky State Police (Retired)

- **Peter Callinicos**, Instructor, Emergency and Public Service, Red Rocks Community College, Lakewood, Colorado, and Captain (Retired), Denver Fire Department

- **James Hatch**, City Manager, Walker, Michigan

- **Marvin Herrington**, Chief of Police (Retired), Stanford University, Stanford, California

- **Leslie G. Horne, Jr.**, Loss Prevention Manager, Texas Municipal League Intergovernmental Risk Pool

- **Doug Kirkus**, Loss Control Manager, Risk Services of South Dakota

- **Daniel S. McDevitt**, Chief of Police, Lansing Police Department, Lansing, Illinois

- **Stephen D. McGinn**, R.M.P.E., Director of Policyholder Relations, Florida League of Cities, Inc.

- **Frederick Ryan**, Chief of Police, Arlington Police Department, Arlington, Massachusetts

About the Authors

Vincent F. Faggiano

Vincent F. Faggiano served for thirty-two years with the Rochester Police Department, Rochester, New York. During that time, he rose through the ranks and retired as the Commander of the Patrol Division. He has also served as the commander of the Monroe County Drug Task Force, which was responsible for providing drug enforcement service to all jurisdictions in Monroe County.

Vince has trained thousands of police supervisors, fire command officers, emergency medical technicians, community leaders, elected officials, and others to respond to critical incidents in their communities. He was selected by the U.S. Department of Justice to deliver this program to the Panamanian National Police Force and members of the presidential cabinet after "Operation Just Cause" reinstated a democratic government in Panama. His national experience provides first-hand knowledge of problems other communities have encountered and the solutions they have found.

In his spare time, Vince founded the police band, *Lightning*, through which he has donated thousands of hours to encourage youngsters to remain drug-free. He composed the songs "Just Say No" and "Do the Right Thing," the official theme song for the national D.A.R.E. program.

Along with numerous awards for his service to the community, Vince received the Rochester Police Department's highest award, the Medal of Valor, for lifesaving actions taken during a barricaded gunman/hostage situation.

Thomas T. Gillespie

Thomas T. Gillespie began his law enforcement career in Detroit, Michigan in 1970 and worked as a patrol officer and as a sergeant-field supervisor. During 1971-1974 Tom served in the US Army as a military police officer and subsequently with the Army's Criminal Investigation Division. Tom returned to Detroit after his military service and in 1979 was selected to serve as the Chief of Police for the City of Las Vegas (New Mexico) Police Department. In 1984 he became the Director of the New Mexico Law Enforcement Academy as well as the Director of the New Mexico Department of Public Safety Training & Recruiting Division. Tom then served as Director of the State of New Mexico Attorney General's Investigative Division.

In 1987 Tom began offering training and consulting services as the owner of Criminal Justice Training & Consulting Services (CJTC). Through CJTC, Tom conducts agency management audits, policy and procedure development, management of the investigative function programs, entry level and promotional process, strategic and project planning seminars, and executive and supervisory training programs. Tom has provided training for the US Department of Justice and the US Department of State, conducting programs in several countries in Central and South America.

Since 1990 Tom has delivered more than 400 critical incident training programs in 36 states, training over 8,000 law enforcement, fire, and paramedic personnel in initial response and executive command post operations. These programs have been delivered in partnership with BowMac Educational Services, Inc., Honeoye Falls, NY.

Tom offers expert witness consultation and testimony and has been qualified as a law enforcement expert in both State and Federal Court. He has been retained in over 300 civil and criminal actions. Tom is also the co-author of *Police Use of Force: A Line Officer's Guide*.

Foreword

by

Daniel S. McDevitt
Chief of Police
Lansing Police Department
Lansing, Illinois

I am both flattered and privileged to write the foreword for what I consider to be a very important text.

By way of background, I have been a law enforcement professional since 1974 and have worked for agencies at the federal, state, county, and local levels. I am also a retired Military Intelligence Officer and serve as an instructor for three universities. I have provided law enforcement and management training throughout the U.S. and overseas for military and civilian law enforcement personnel. As you can imagine, I have been through many, many training programs over the years.

In December 1998, while a Captain with the Illinois State Police, I was required to attend a week-long Critical Incident Management course taught by the authors of this book, Tom Gillespie and Vinny Faggiano. Thinking that this would be "just another school," I approached the week with a fair amount of skepticism. (Many years in law enforcement have a tendency to make one somewhat skeptical)

I can honestly say that the course was, without question, the single best course I have ever attended in my career, before or since. It quickly became apparent that Tom and Vinny are more than just gifted instructors. Their vast backgrounds in law enforcement have earned them the credibility to be able to provide this type of training to their fellow cops, firefighters, and other public safety personnel. And as you know, credibility for an instructor or an author is something that public safety personnel do not take lightly.

There is more than enough information in this book for even the novice law enforcement supervisor to be able to fully function at a variety of critical incidents. There is an excellent section on "Critical Incident Stress" that many similar texts overlook completely. Perhaps the most important chapter is on the Seven Critical Tasks, complete with easy to understand diagrams. I have used the Seven Critical Tasks during several incidents, and I can assure you that they really do work.

Having carefully read this book, I am willing to put my nearly thirty year law enforcement reputation on the line when I state the following:

A careful examination of this book, coupled with adaptation of the suggested practices and tactics, will provide any public safety practitioner and supervisor with the tools needed to address and successfully manage any type of critical incident.

Contents

Introduction

Pop quiz time: It's been a quiet night shift. You're heading back to the station to close out when you receive a call on a motor vehicle accident. With no other information available, it seems routine. You roll up on scene only to find a school bus full of children overturned and wrapped around a ruptured tanker truck. What immediate actions do you take? What resources will you need?

Critical incidents usually happen when you least expect them. But they needn't happen when you're least prepared.

That's where this book comes in. It gives law enforcement first responders a workable game plan for handling the unexpected. Since 1990, the authors have provided critical incident management instruction to thousands of responders and supervisors around the country. Time and time again, students have praised the practical information provided in these programs for its simplicity and effectiveness.

All critical incidents share some common characteristics. The basic premise of this book is that, if critical incidents have common characteristics, we can establish a common set of response strategies to address these characteristics. There are certain steps or tasks you can always apply at the onset of a critical incident to quickly and effectively manage the scene. Of course the incident elements will vary from scene to scene, but the core tasks remain the same regardless of the type of event you face.

While no book can replace training and experience, the information provided here will give you a major head start on understanding basic management tasks. These guidelines lead you through every phase of a critical incident: from taking initial scene command, to managing resources, and finally to resolving the incident.

Who Should Read This Book?

This book is geared toward law enforcement responders. There are issues unique to police response that simply do not apply to fire and EMS. Which is not to say that these pages will not discuss integrating with other agencies: that is a critical component of major incident response.

Whether you are a seasoned officer or a newly promoted sergeant, this information will improve your ability and confidence to manage any type of major incident.

The old pro will recognize many of the book's recommendations as part of their current management style, but he or she will gain valuable information from our examination of various types of critical incidents. The new sergeant has the opportunity to learn from the experiences—both good and bad—of thousands of law enforcement supervisors who have managed critical events.

As well as applying to all incident types, the tasks and techniques discussed in this book apply to all types of law enforcement agencies. A large urban police or federal agency may have numerous resources available for a prompt response, but it is the proper *management* of these resources that is crucial to incident stabilization. The only difference for the rural sheriff's office is that a first responder may have to wait a few minutes longer for support. You will quickly find that when it comes to critical incident response, the actions you must initiate are similar for all sizes and types of law enforcement agencies.

Appropriate Response

The initial actions taken by a first-responding supervisor determine whether a critical incident is allowed to accelerate out of control or is quickly stabilized. Law enforcement officers are usually first to the scene in the vast majority of critical incidents. You will read this repeatedly: It's up to *you* to make decisions and take early, appropriate action.

In most cases you will not know that you are responding to a major incident until your unit rolls up on scene. Critical incidents are not reported as such. A seemingly routine call can quickly escalate into a major critical event. For example:

- One of the first calls received in the 1999 Columbine high school tragedy in Littleton, Colorado was to check for a student down in the parking lot.

- In the 1993 bombing of the World Trade Center, the initial emergency call came in as a transformer fire.

The point is not so much "always expect the unexpected" as to simply be prepared to implement a strong response plan if called upon.

The following chapters will examine various types of critical incidents. If you implement the "game plan" outlined in this book, you improve your ability to limit the growth of those incidents and stabilize your scenes.

NIMS and ICS

Let's look at the big picture for a moment. The National Incident Management System (NIMS) is a federally mandated program of incident response, training, and publications. NIMS represents a national policy for critical incident response. Its recommendations and guidelines provide a framework for coordinating federal, state, and local resources.

A primary component of NIMS (and of any critical incident response) is the Incident Command System (ICS). This book is *not* a theoretical discussion of NIMS and ICS. Although you will read about ICS components and implementation, it will be in a real-world context: You pulling up on the scene of a school bus/tanker truck accident with limited resources at 0800 on a foggy and rainy morning.

But make no mistake: even if you are a patrol officer, if you are the first on-scene at an incident, *you are in command.*

Somebody has to be. It will be you or nobody until a supervisor can relieve you.

This book will introduce you to the primary functional areas of NIMS and some of the requirements incumbent on you as a critical incident commander. Critical incident management, and particularly crisis phase management, is the working end of the whole NIMS/ICS structure. The point of the spear, if you will. It's where these high-level concepts meet the barricaded terrorist and the ruptured tanker car. It's where *you* make the whole system work.

Figure I-1: Critical incident management is an integral part of larger national response plans. It's where the rubber meets the road.

The Importance of Training

This book will focus on two phases of critical incident supervision: **crisis response** and **scene management**. You'll learn how to assess an event and order and deploy resources effectively. Of course, your organization may have plans in place for certain events. But appropriate response is more than just planning:

> *A plan is only as good as the training that backs it up! You must educate yourself and your department to implement appropriate critical incident response.*

We can give you an overview of the issues you will face and the thought processes you must go through, but a book is no substitute for training and training is no substitute for experience. Would you attempt a SWAT assault after reading one book on the subject? Of course not. You must practice the tasks and techniques outlined in this book on a regular basis.

Most responding officers "flashback" on similar incidents they've handled to guide their actions. But if you've never managed a critical incident, you have only your training to rely on. Get it if you can. And make sure it's as realistic as possible.

Our classroom training, for example, involves complex scenarios played out on a large model city. Each participant must manage an incident in front of the others in the class—frequently their agency peers. Many of our students have told us that the incidents they managed on the model city were more difficult than real-life critical events with which they've been involved. It's only through training and experience that a plan can be expected to actually work in the field.

What You'll Find Inside

Over the next several chapters you'll be introduced to a unique law enforcement perspective on critical incident management. Much of it is common sense, but other recommendations are a departure from traditional response strategies. If you are like thousands of others, you will find the information thought-provoking and easy to implement.

- You are not alone. The first chapter discusses many of the issues identified by our students over the years as having impacted their responses. Subsequently, each concern is addressed with problem-solving techniques and winning attitudes.

- You will read about the common stages of a critical incident (from crisis to termination) and the tasks you must implement to stabilize the scene. And because all cops are storytellers, you'll find real-life incidents throughout the book to reinforce concepts.

- What makes a good tactical leader? You'll learn the leadership style and techniques required to manage a critical incident successfully in the early crisis phase.

- There are tasks you must always do and do quickly. These "Seven Critical Tasks" serve as your game plan for managing any type of critical incident.

- From the crisis phase we jump back to the federal level. We will briefly introduce you to NIMS and describe in some detail the flexibility and importance of ICS.

- We all know the world is full of dangerous chemicals that can seriously injure or kill you and the public through accidental or deliberate release. Chapter Six provides need-to-know information about responding to hazardous materials and weapons of mass destruction incidents.

- Lastly, the book examines critical incident stress management. If not identified and handled properly, acute or cumulative stress can have devastating effects on responders.

As you can see, we'll be covering a lot of information. Critical incident response is a complex topic. You as the response leader are under pressure from all sides and frequently under intense public and professional scrutiny to take decisive action. You get only one chance to do the job right.

Throughout this book we reference incidents that you may have read about or perhaps even been involved in. Understand that it is never our intent to criticize or critique agency responses. We perform analyses based exclusively on official reports. This is how law enforcement continually learns from its experience.

We have tremendous respect for first responders who take charge of critical incidents. We've all had to make tough and immediate decisions with little information and high risk. Our passion for this topic is fueled by the belief that the information contained in this book will save lives—those of first responders and citizens. There is no more important purpose.

Vincent F. Faggiano
Thomas T. Gillespie

One

The Nature of Critical Incidents

Objectives

After completing this chapter, you should be able to:

- *Recall the most common characteristics of critical incident response*

- *Describe the three universal criteria for agency response plans*

- *Recognize the impact of politics (external, internal, and interagency) on agency response*

- *Differentiate between uncontrollable and controllable incident factors*

So what is a critical incident? This book uses a broad definition that covers every conceivable type of occurrence:

A critical incident is an extraordinary event that
places lives and property in danger and requires the
commitment and coordination of numerous resources
to bring about a successful conclusion.

You can probably recall a few responses that fit this definition. It is deliberately inclusive. Within the critical incident category, there are several types of events that you could be called upon to manage. A short list includes the following:

- **Terrorist Activities (Weapons of Mass Destruction)**—For the range of weapons of mass destruction, think B-NICE: biological, nuclear, incendiary, chemical, and explosive.

- **Natural Disasters**—You will have your hands full in the event of earthquake, hurricane, tornado, flood, ice storm, or blizzard.

- **Transportation Accidents**—These range from fender benders to mass-casualty bus accidents and train derailments. This category also includes plane crashes and shipping mishaps. Each jurisdiction has its own hazards. Additionally, any transportation accident has the potential to involve hazardous materials.

- **Criminal Activities**—This broad category can include bombings, active shooters, barricaded gunmen, and hostage situations.

- **Fires/Hazardous Materials Incidents**—Chemical spills and explosions, industrial fires, high-rise and multiple dwelling fires can quickly become the most dangerous events of all. In the vast majority of hazmat situations, a police officer is the first on-scene.

That's a wide range of incident types, but they have more in common than most people would imagine.

Common Characteristics

As we mentioned in the introduction, since 1990 we have had the opportunity to share the management strategies discussed in this book with thousands of emergency responders. Participants have included:

- Law enforcement personnel from patrol officers to police chiefs

- Fire service supervisors from lieutenants to chiefs

- Emergency medical technicians and supervisors

- State, local, and federal authorities

- Emergency management personnel

In one classroom exercise, students identify common issues that have caused them problems in managing critical incidents, especially in the crisis phase. The similarities among the lists from each session are truly amazing. Geography doesn't matter. Agency representatives from every corner of the United States and beyond identify the same issues. Think the size of your organization makes a difference? Similar issues apply regardless of whether respondents work in small, mid-size, or large departments—rural or urban, for that matter.

Most interestingly, responses are generally the same regardless of the *specific nature* of the incident. It does not matter what type of incident you face. The issues described in this chapter apply equally to all, be they natural disasters, barricaded gunmen, hazardous material spills, or mass casualty incidents.

Common issues fall into the following broad categories:

- Communications

- Who's in charge?

- Resources and resource coordination

- Intelligence gathering and problem assessment

- Crowd and traffic control (perimeters)

- Environment

- Planning and training

- The media

- Politics

As you read through these, think of an incident you have responded to. Try to recall if any or all of the identified issues had an impact—positive or negative—on your response.

Communications

Communications encompasses so many areas that responders almost always identify it as the number one issue that impacts their incident response. Specifically, concerns usually break out into technical, personal, and organizational communication.

Line officers and supervisors usually identify communications concerns in terms of equipment or technical issues such as:

- Poor radio equipment

- Lack of quality power sources (i.e., batteries dying in the field)

- Lack of a common radio frequency that can be shared by all responders

- Garbled or unreadable transmissions from the scene due to poor reception or transmission (weak signals and dead spots)

Obviously, any equipment issues can have a direct effect on problem assessment and deployment of personnel to stabilize the scene. What can you do to limit technical communications problems on-scene? Prepare. Plan. Procure!

Personal communication issues, such as the ability to communicate effectively in spite of the high-stress conditions at the scene, are also identified as key. Can you organize your thoughts and give critical orders under pressure? We will discuss leadership issues, including tactical communication, in the "Who's in Charge?" section on the next page and in Chapter Three (see page 43).

Administrative personnel tend to identify organizational communication issues that go beyond technical considerations. These issues can have as great or greater impact at a scene. These concerns include:

- Departmental sharing of expectations with responders

- Communication of response plans to those responsible for implementing the plans

- Communication with other responding agencies— other law enforcement agencies as well as fire, EMS, etc.

- Use of Ten Codes

All of the areas listed above directly impact the effectiveness of the first responding units. Do you know what your organization expects of you in a crisis? Do you know what plans are available? Can your organization effectively coordinate with fire and EMS? Most of these issues touch on training, which we will address shortly.

It is easy to see why communications can have the single greatest impact on the initial response to a critical incident. Doubtless, you can recall many instances in which communications (both good and bad) affected your response.

Who's in Charge?

The dilemma of command turns up in every problem assessment exercise. This is cited as a major issue at *every* scene—even in single-agency responses! The standard answer to the question, "Who's in charge?" is a simple one: "You are!" Clarity of command—to those on-scene and those involved off-site, such as dispatchers—is imperative to prevent confusion and the potentially tragic results that confusion can cause.

Multiple-agency and multi-*disciplinary* (police, fire, and EMS) responses add a whole new spin to the command issue.

Of course, the question of a scene's overall management and the assumption of command can be complex. In Chapter Five (see page 95), we will discuss implementing a "unified command" structure as outlined in the national ICS model. For response to an incident in the crisis phase, however, use a much simpler approach: Each discipline is in charge of and responsible for its own particular area of expertise.

Simply put, the folks with the hoses are responsible for fire suppression. The folks with the ambulances and medical equipment are responsible for treatment and victim transport. Law enforcement is responsible for traffic and crowd control, site security, and police-related activities.

Focus on your tasks. Don't make command more complicated than it has to be.

Resources and Resource Coordination

Not surprisingly, when participants talk about resources as a problem, what they usually mean is that they *lack* resources. Such a lack may well hamper the initial management of a spontaneous critical incident. Expect your initial response to be less than what you need or request.

An unusual characteristic of critical incidents, however, is that the lack of resources in the crisis phase of an incident is usually offset by an *enormous* resource response in a very short period of time. This applies whether you are in an urban or a rural setting. Your ability to shift gears from directing an understaffed response to directing a large response is an essential part of effective critical incident management.

When we do not coordinate resources in a major response efficiently, our management appears unorganized, disjointed, and confused. The arrival of resources requires us to bring order to chaos. The ICS discussion later will provide a time-tested method to accomplish this feat. Also, one of the Seven Critical Tasks is devoted to establishing a staging area for responding resources. This is a central location where resources wait to be assigned duties by the scene supervisor.

Intelligence Gathering and Problem Assessment

There are questions that you need answered at any incident scene:

- What happened?

- What am I dealing with?

- What are the dangers?

- What can impact and worsen this scene?

- What needs to be done to stabilize and resolve this incident?

The decisions you make depend on the availability and quality of the answers to these questions. And in turn, your ability to *get* answers, and the *quality* of those answers, is affected by the panic and confusion that characterize the crisis phase of an incident. Add to that the urgency to take action during the crisis phase, and intelligence gathering may become your most difficult task.

We will discuss the need for good problem assessment skills on the part of the first responding crisis manager in the following chapters. Poor problem assessment or intelligence gathering will result in poor decision making and may inflame a situation rather than stabilizing or resolving it.

The better your intelligence, of course, the more informed and appropriate your decisions will be.

Crowd and Traffic Control (Perimeters)

We must limit access to a scene and prevent gridlock. It is our responsibility to prevent unwitting individuals from endangering themselves by entering areas that may pose a threat to their safety. We must also provide a controlled area that allows emergency workers to perform their duties unimpeded by bystanders or crowds.

The term "crowd" applies to swarms of emergency responders as well as civilians. A scene gridlocked by a mob of emergency workers is just as inaccessible as a scene gridlocked by a mob of civilians. It is our responsibility to provide both access and egress for a scene. Exerting crowd and traffic control by establishing perimeters is without question one of the primary law enforcement tasks at any emergency scene.

Environment

This one may seem pretty obvious, but it needs to be mentioned. As you will see shortly, critical incidents are made up of controllable and noncontrollable factors. Weather and the area in which you encounter an incident are definitely uncontrollable. However, since most of our responses are outdoors, we must all contend with our environments!

You may work in rain, fog, snow, blazing heat, or dust storms. You may be on the plains or a cliff, in the desert or in swampland. Regardless, you must manage *around* the environmental conditions in your jurisdiction.

Take into account the impact weather and topography may have on your planning and your resource requirements, such as communications and shelter. At a minimum, you must protect your command post from the elements. It's hard to make calm, informed decisions while shielding your face from driving sleet.

Planning and Training

The planning an agency does to organize and prepare for critical incidents is a key first step to having a viable response strategy. Although planning is critical, it is effective only if responders understand and can implement those plans.

Agencies often spend hundreds of hours developing specific plans for specific incidents. It is not unusual for an agency to have a barricaded gunman plan, a hostage plan, a hazardous material spill plan, an airplane crash response plan, a natural disaster response plan, and so on.

What can that leave you with? Notebooks upon notebooks filled with orders and procedures. These are great for evaluating an agency's response post-incident, but may not be exactly accessible by the newly promoted sergeant working the midnight shift. Are your plans fully understood and capable of being implemented?

Plans must be able to make the transition from the tranquility of the administrative offices where they are conceived to the chaos of a critical incident in the field where they are used. Therefore they should be simple, flexible, and clearly understandable by field personnel. Strategies must be tested through training and practical application.

It continues to amaze: We in law enforcement take an area with the greatest ramifications—the potential life and death of our responders and the public—and do little or no related training. Then we expect our people to perform well under the most trying conditions imaginable. We fail to train with our counterpart fire and EMS responders, but we are expected to integrate our tactics and strategies with them in a unified response. This must change.

It is imperative that all agency plans meet the following criteria:

- The plan must be simple

- All responders must understand the plan

- All responders must practice that plan through scenario training

The rest of the information in this book, particularly the Seven Critical Tasks, will provide the fundamental steps you can apply to any situation.

The Media

Reporters are drawn to critical incidents like bears to honey. Traditionally, our profession has not incorporated media representatives into emergency response. The media has therefore been left on their own to gain information and report on events. As a result of their independent actions, there have been occasions when they have been counterproductive to resolving critical incidents. We have all been on or heard of scenes where media coverage was incomplete or inaccurate. At other scenes, members of the media have been an intrusive presence that simply added to the work of responders.

As we will see later, it doesn't have to be this way. There have been numerous occasions in which the media has been well-informed and incorporated into emergency response plans. AMBER Alerts are a good example.

Politics

Many consider politics too sensitive for official discussion in a classroom or response book. We feel politics is a topic too important *not* to be discussed. It is something that field personnel feel they should not have to consider, yet it frequently dominates the thoughts of their upper-level command officers.

Simply put, if a field commander has a tactical solution to a problem, but that solution is politically unacceptable, that commander does not have a solution.

You can think of politics as falling into three broad categories, each having the potential to impact a critical incident response:

- Traditional external political influences brought about by elected officials, community members, or others outside our specific agency
- Internal politics within our own agency
- Interagency politics

Regarding **external politics**, a basic tenet of American civilian policing is that we serve and protect the communities that hire us. Therefore, we are answerable to those communities and their elected officials. Such external influences are an undeniable factor of critical incident management. This is especially true during the "executive management" phase of a critical response, which we will get into in the next chapter.

As a critical incident supervisor, the overall quality of the relationship between your department and your jurisdictional government is probably not your direct responsibility. Hopefully, it's a good working relationship. If each department member does his or her job professionally, there should be no cause for friction.

Never underestimate the impact of **internal politics**. Agencies in turmoil and/or transition tend to respond differently to critical incidents than stable organizations. Individuals vying for recognition or "jockeying for position" can bring hidden agendas to the management team. This can manifest itself in a variety of ways, from inappropriate assumption of command to unjustifiable decision-making at the scene. Any ulterior motive beyond public and responder safety can greatly jeopardize a response. (And lead to external political problems!)

Departments rarely discuss or acknowledge these internal conditions. Instead, gossip grinds through the rumor mill and can have a destructive effect on both morale and confidence.

If these conditions exist within your organization, the top management team must be willing to recognize, acknowledge, and minimize their impact on your agency's response. This responsibility falls *squarely* upon the upper level command staff. Failure to address the distractions of internal politics can have disastrous effects on both the organization and the community.

And lastly, **interagency politics** have a long and storied history. If you've been around for a while, you've probably seen the effects of tension among local, state, and federal agencies. The issues are to numerous to deal with here, but most problems can be addressed with a few simple techniques:

- **Focus on the scene.** You and your mutual response agencies all want the same thing: a swift and safe resolution. Keep your eye on what's best for incident response.

- **Ignore personality issues.** Don't give in to personal antagonism for someone you find abrasive or with whom you've had difficulties in the past.

- **Recognize competence.** Other agencies may have special competencies to deal with your situation. Give them the benefit of the doubt.

You have your own areas of competence, which may include a more detailed knowledge of an incident scene or participants. Work *with* responders from other agencies. Don't work against them or give them reason to work against you.

It is often said that from tragedy good things may flow. There is now widespread recognition that we need to work cooperatively should our communities come under attack. We have seen first-hand the crumbling of barriers that have existed for years. Organizations that have not traditionally interacted well are now training together and will therefore be better prepared to respond together. We can no longer allow petty differences to compromise the protection of our communities.

Uncontrollable vs. Controllable Factors

Needless to say, a critical incident can happen any time, any place, without warning. Incidents accelerate or decelerate based on a variety of uncontrollable and controllable factors. It is your job as a first responder to focus on the aspects *you* can control. Remember, the less time an incident has to develop, the more likely you are to gain control of the scene.

We all know that elements beyond our control can greatly impact (and in some cases determine) our strategies. You will not be able to change the **uncontrollable factors** listed on the next page, but you can make informed decisions to lessen their impact.

- **Time.** Day or night? In the middle of rush hour, perhaps? If at night, you may need to obtain portable lights to manage the scene effectively.

- **Weather.** Sunny and dry, or sleeting, snowing, and foggy? A balmy 70°, a sweltering 102°, or a very frigid -5°? The safety and well-being of your officers is *your* responsibility. If it's cold or raining, make sure your personnel have proper equipment to allow them to do their jobs. If it's 120° on the asphalt, make sure those directing traffic have access to shade, fluids, and frequent relief.

- **Location.** Are you operating in an urban environment or do you find yourself miles from the nearest stoplight? What kind of terrain are you dealing with? You could be in the flats or looking down at a school bus at the bottom of a 50-foot ravine. Once on-scene, you need to quickly assess obstacles and call for the proper resources to deal with them.

- **Initial injuries/death.** Certainly, a large number of injuries or deaths can impact you and your responders. All you can do is try to keep a situation from deteriorating. Your job is to reduce further harm.

- **Weapons.** Concerns include the number of weapons, the caliber, whether they are semi or fully automatic, and whether any heavier ordnance is involved. You may find yourself "out-gunned" at a scene. When this happens, your first job is to ensure the safety of your people: back them off, get them behind proper cover. Then order up appropriate reinforcement.

- **Chemicals.** If you respond to the scene of a hazmat spill, the agents involved could be toxic, poisonous, corrosive, explosive…the list is depressingly long. You must quickly determine the type of chemical and take action to protect your personnel and citizens.

A key theme of this book is that you must focus your energies on **controllable factors**. In the early stages of an incident, these are the elements that can make or break your response. They include the following:

- **Access to the scene.** It's up to you to prevent gridlock caused by the public and a potentially overwhelming emergency response. Make sure *your* personnel have proper access and do not contribute to gridlock. This involves establishing proper perimeters and a staging area.

- **Limiting crowd size.** The task of controlling crowds for their safety is a primary police function. You can expect crowds at any critical incident. You must make sure those crowds do not become unmanageable. This is especially applicable to civil disturbances. While you may not be able to control the size of the crowd before your arrival, you certainly want to limit others from joining in once you establish scene control.

- **Evacuating adjacent areas.** Most critical incidents involve threat to civilians in the immediate area. If evacuation is not an option, you may "shelter-in-place" homes, businesses, and facilities such as schools and hospitals. The sooner you define who might be endangered and protect them from harm, the quicker you will be able to stabilize the scene.

- **Rerouting traffic flow.** You must swiftly ensure the safety of motorists and others in the area. If possible, keep traffic flowing some distance from the scene. Your perimeters must be far enough away from the incident to ensure citizen and responder safety but close enough so that you can effectively manage citizen and responder movement. In other words, don't establish an outer perimeter that you don't have the resources to control.

- **Ordering additional personnel and equipment.** Try to recognize potential resource needs as soon as possible. Err on the side of caution: If you think you might need additional resources or support from other agencies, get them rolling. Specialists such as hazmat or SWAT teams usually won't arrive immediately. An early request will reduce their response time to the scene.

- **Where and how you use your personnel.** You must take charge. As the leader, you allocate and position resources as you see fit. Make sure your decisions contribute to the stabilization of the scene. If all of your people are helping EMS personnel rescue injured persons at a mass casualty incident, you may be neglecting perimeter control and allowing road and foot traffic into what you will come to know as the kill zone. We call this focusing on "resolution" rather than "stabilization" during the crisis phase of an incident.

- **Establishing communication with personnel.** Unless you are experiencing technical difficulties, it's up to you to maintain communication with all responders on the scene. Make sure they know what you expect from them. The best laid plan can be quickly compromised by a shot fired in error or a unit simply moving out of position without orders.

- **Your own command presence.** Your ability to take charge and issue clear and concise orders is crucial. The decisions you make and your attitudes dictate events and the response of your subordinates.

Summary

As you've read through this chapter, did you compare the issues raised against your own critical incident experience? If you have, you undoubtedly found many of the issues familiar.

Knowing the potential hurdles is the first step to overcoming them. Focus on the factors you can control and work around those you can't. And remember: you are not alone. *We all face the same issues.*

Review Questions

1. Can you recall several of the most common obstacles to critical incident response?

2. Can you state the three universal "usability" criteria for agency response plans?

3. Can you differentiate between internal, external, and interagency politics?

4. Can you explain the difference between controllable and uncontrollable incident factors?

Two

Response Phases and Strategies

Objectives

After completing this chapter, you should be able to:

- *Identify the main characteristics of each incident phase*

- *Identify the response goals for each incident phase*

- *Identify the appropriate strategies for each incident phase*

All critical incidents—from hostage situations to hazmat releases—share certain common traits. An analysis of hundreds of incidents has shown that major events can progress through four distinct phases. Each phase has unique characteristics and each requires special management skills. This chapter discusses the characteristics of each of those phases, along with strategies you can use and the outcomes you can expect. The table on the following two pages provides an overview of the information that we will cover in detail.

Crisis ❯ Scene Management ❯ Executive Management ❯ Termination

Figure 2-1: Major events progress through each incident phase. Smaller incidents may not require executive management or even scene management.

Incident Phases	**Crisis**	**Scene Management**
Typical Duration	0 to 60 minutes	Hours to several days
Characteristics	• Confusion • Panic • Rush to scene • Gridlock	• Potential for danger continues • Continuation of incident for longer duration • Arrival of crowds, resources, and media • Requires increased management
Goals	• Stabilize the scene • Limit acceleration and growth of the incident • Ensure citizen and responder safety	• Establish an organized decision-making team with ICS to bring about a safe and successful resolution of the event
Response Strategies	• Initiate tactical management style • First responding supervisor initiates 7 Critical Tasks • Identify initial ICS functions needed • Evaluate resource requirements • Evaluate evacuation and/ or shelter-in-place requirements	• Select site for scene/field command post • Expand ICS with specific functions • Develop and implement incident action plan • Evaluate resource requirements • Assess communications requirements • Initiate evacuation plan (if required) • Deploy specialists to bring about incident resolution
Outcomes *If not resolved:* *Move to next phase* *If resolved:* *move to Termination phase*	• Safety of citizens and responders is provided • Scene stabilized • Proactive management of scene to move ahead of incident acceleration	• A unified command structure is established (if required) • An organized decision-making team with ICS is established

Executive Management	Termination
Several hours, a week or longer	Accomplished over several days or weeks
Size, scope and seriousness of the event is beyond the ability of scene/field command post to manage	• Incident resolved • Order restored
• Establish a fully expanded Incident Command System to bring about a safe and successful resolution of the event	• Ensure scene integrity • Bring about a smooth transition to normal operations • Improve agency response to the next critical incident • Maintain emotional and physical well-being of the organization

• Establish Emergency Operations Center (EOC) by expanding ICS
• Establish unified command structure (if required)
• Appointment of the IC is determined by the nature of incident, by the type of resources required, and through policy and/or legal authority
• Evaluate current incident action plan and update as appropriate
• Support field operations
• Review and evaluate evacuation plan
	• Implement plan for returning to normal operations
	  - Account for all personnel
	  - Assess damage/injuries
	  - Reassign personnel
	• Re-establish evacuated areas
	• Conduct tactical review
	• Conduct stress debriefing and provide counseling
	• Prepare after-action reports
	• Review policy and assess training needs:
	  - What happened?
	  - What was our response?
	  - What would we do differently next time?

• A fully expanded Incident Command System brings about an organized team approach for the safe and successful resolution of the event	• Event activity and agency response is properly documented • Information is provided that will benefit the profession • Opportunities are provided for all personnel to receive assistance with any emotional and/or physical needs

Regardless of the specific nature of an incident, every one includes (at a minimum) a crisis phase and a termination phase. Other incidents evolve from crisis to the scene management phase and eventually to termination. In the case of catastrophic events, such as natural disasters, a high-level executive management phase may also be required.

Crisis Phase

It's 0630 hours, the end of a quiet night shift. You're on your way back to the station when dispatch notifies you of an MVA with confirmed injuries. Your first car on-scene advises that he has a school bus versus tanker truck. The tanker is leaking an unknown liquid that may be forming a gas cloud.

Several children appear to be trapped in the overturned bus. Three passersby, apparently not involved in the accident, are down and unmoving. Both the bus driver and tanker driver are dead or unconscious. Traffic is snarled in all directions.

You are in the crisis phase. What are you going to do to contain the situation? What questions do you need answered? What resources are you going to need?

All critical incidents share certain common characteristics at the outset. In the first 30 minutes or so, the crisis phase, you can expect confusion and panic on the part of the public. Criminal activity involving gunfire or explosions, for example, may create mass movement away from the incident. Motorists on the event fringes may slow down to see what's going on. At the same time, you and other responders will be rushing to the scene as quickly as possible.

The result is gridlock. The public acts blindly on little or no information until you, as the scene commander, can determine the nature of the situation and exert control. You must bring order to chaos. Confusion in the early moments can greatly hinder your ability to determine just what you're facing. Responding units and agencies may add to the confusion if you do not manage their response.

A critical incident compresses and accelerates all of your order, planning, and decision-making processes, especially when you are operating in a dangerous environment. The threat can come from a rolling gas cloud or by gunfire. Others, such as the survivors of a bus or plane crash, may be in imminent danger. You don't have the luxury of conducting a meeting with other supervisors to discuss strategies...you must take action. Failure to act may lead the incident to accelerate out of control.

When you respond, you *must have a plan*. You can't rely on your ability to make it up as you go along. And as we pointed out in the previous chapter, that plan must have been tested through training.

Initial Objectives and Strategies

Your initial goals are to limit the growth of the incident, ensure the safety of both civilians and responders, and stabilize the scene. You have to take action to make sure the situation doesn't get worse before you can move toward resolution. Remember, the less time an incident has to develop in the crisis phase, the greater your opportunities to stabilize it.

How do you achieve this? A critical first step is to adopt a tactical command presence at the scene. You must assume command and announce it over the available communication channel. This simple practice, long used by the fire service, has not been embraced by law enforcement. A short radio communication establishing command clarifies on-scene authority for the dispatcher, your responding units, and other mutual aid resources directed to assist at the scene.

In the parlance of the Incident Command System (ICS), you become the Incident Commander (IC). The IC collects the best available information and makes necessary decisions. Acting as an IC in the crisis phase of an incident requires a different management style than you probably use day-to-day. This is referred to as the difference between "tactical" and "traditional" leadership styles.

Briefly, a tactical leader must be autocratic. You issue immediate and specific orders. Be aware that in a crisis, autocratic leadership rarely creates resentment. Rather, the reverse is true: subordinates and civilians faced with a crisis situation rely on the direction only a confident IC can provide. If you act with confidence and decisiveness, your subordinates will too.

The first-responding supervisor or scene commander takes action to stabilize the situation and preserve life and property. Because most critical incidents share common characteristics, it follows that you can use a set of common responses for bringing those incidents under control. These are known as the Seven Critical Tasks. The tasks are:

1. Establish control and communications

2. Identify the kill zone

3. Establish the inner perimeter

4. Establish the outer perimeter

5. Establish the on-scene command post

6. Establish a staging area

7. Identify and request additional resources

Even though the tasks are numbered, that does not mean they must be done in that particular sequence. You can perform them in whatever order is appropriate for your incident. Regardless of the order, these steps represent your "game plan" for managing the crisis phase of any type of critical incident. We will cover these crucial tasks in detail in Chapter Four (see page 55).

Let's recap the functions of a first-responding supervisor in the crisis phase:

- Stabilize and limit the growth of the incident

- Ensure the safety of citizens and responders

- Take action to gain control of the scene, including preparing the scene for the entry of specialists (SWAT, bomb tech, hazmat, fire, search and rescue, and so on)

Outcomes

So what can happen at the conclusion of the crisis phase? As you might expect, events can go a couple of different ways. The incident may resolve itself at this stage. If your gunman surrenders, you would proceed to the "termination" phase of incident management.

This may happen, but it is *not a primary goal* for the crisis stage. *Not* seeking immediate resolution is a major departure from traditional incident response training. This is a key difference between the approach outlined in this book and traditional methodologies. In the past, we have been taught to go in and resolve a situation as quickly as possible. Years of hard experience have taught us that your primary goals need to be *limiting incident growth, stabilizing the scene, and ensuring the safety of responders and citizens.*

Early stabilization, rather than resolution, is a difficult concept for laymen to grasp. In our opinion, the response to the Columbine high school tragedy in 1999 was unfairly criticized by non-responders for this very reason. On-scene supervisors in that case acted with restraint and focused on incident control, stabilization, and intelligence gathering in the crisis phase. If responding agencies had acted without information and without control of the scene, that event could have been much, much worse.

You must beware of the "tunnel vision" that can lead you to focus on resolution in the crisis phase. You may be provoked to act impetuously and without information. This focus can allow a situation to escalate out of control. You *must* stabilize the scene first.

It is extremely unlikely your incident will be resolved in the crisis phase. But even if the incident is not resolved, you should at least have accomplished the three goals outlined in this section.

For example, you might still have a gunman barricaded in the house, but you have perimeters established and have taken other steps that allow you to progress to the next phase—"scene management."

Scene Management Phase

Back at the intersection, you've accomplished the Seven Critical Tasks and stabilized the scene. The hardest decision you had to make was to leave the children in the bus for an extended period of time. Based on the placard on the truck, you determined the fluid leaking from the tanker was acetone.

You have evacuated all houses and businesses within two blocks of the intersection. Your command post is in place and you are coordinating with EMS to remove the wounded public and responders. Fire services and hazmat have begun to contain the spill. Concerned parents are arriving at the outer perimeter and clogging your communications center with inquiries about their children's welfare.

Now what do you do?

Once you've stabilized the situation but determined that the threat will continue for some time, you've entered the "scene management" phase. This phase can last anywhere from hours to several days depending on the nature and severity of the incident.

There is still a potential for danger to the public and responders, but the emphasis shifts to increased management. You are, for example, going to have crowds to manage: more spectators will gather and emergency responders will continue to roll up. The media will certainly arrive during this phase.

Initial Objectives and Strategies

This is where you shift gears from stabilization strategies to an extended and proactive management mode that will allow you to gain control of the situation.

You may have already begun the task of establishing a command post in the crisis phase, but scene management cannot take place without a safe location from which to coordinate your response. As you will learn when we get into the discussion of the Seven Critical Tasks, the command post should be between the inner and outer perimeters. In other words, outside the kill zone but in a controlled area well away from crowds.

It is not be necessary for the command post to have an actual view of the incident scene. In fact, being that close can be both dangerous and a distraction from the larger issues you must address, such as coordinating incoming resources. As the Incident Commander, once you establish your command post, *stay there*; that way everyone knows where to find you.

It is possible that authority may shift at this point if a higher-ranking officer responds to the scene. If you have received a "traditional" ICS orientation, you probably learned that the command hand-off must be handled in a face-to-face briefing. This works for the fire service because of its integral team response strategy, which always places a team leader on-scene from the start.

Law enforcement is different. Officers more often than not respond alone and don't have the benefit of a supervisor on-scene from the "get-go." So it's important to keep in mind that a supervisor en route *can* assume authority over an incident. We've had students tell us they can accomplish several tasks from their vehicles while still minutes from the scene. They are thinking about their game plan, requesting support, and relaying commands to the officers currently on location.

That takes us to ICS, the other primary characteristic of the scene management phase. At this point in the incident you have more resources and a new set of problems to handle. ICS is critical for creating a flexible command structure to adapt to these issues as they arise.

Your primary goal in the scene management stage is the establishment of an organized decision-making team. In the parlance of the ICS, this may be a "unified command" consisting of specialists and representatives from each responding agency. This is where you let the men and women with hoses handle the hot stuff and those with the stretchers handle the injured. And by all means, let the responders in the "Level A" suits handle the glowing stuff!

In other words, deploy your specialists and let them do their jobs. Don't micromanage. You cannot make every decision or be everywhere at once. Don't try.

This phase requires that you drop the autocratic leadership style you used in the crisis phase. It would be counterproductive. During scene management you will be working with more departments and specialists and need to revert to the collaborative, empowering management style you probably use day to day.

ICS consists of several functional areas such as operations, intelligence, liaison, safety, and so on. We will go into more detail later, but the beauty of ICS is you need only implement the functions that apply to managing *your* scene. Do you need an information officer to handle the media? If the answer is yes, appoint one (don't do it yourself!). If not, don't worry about that function. It's a "toolbox" approach to incident management. Select the tools you need to accomplish the task at hand.

You need to be flexible in your thinking here. You will be constantly re-evaluating the scene and integrating new ICS functions as necessary:

- If you find yourself managing a major incident, you'll need to appoint an Information Officer to handle the media. Trust us on this one.

- You or a dedicated person will be required to keep a log of the events and decisions as they occur. This is critical for the evaluation that must follow all critical incident responses.

- There may be special considerations. For example, if children are involved you are going to need a liaison to work with the concerned parents who will threaten to inundate and overwhelm your communications center and/or command post.

As the event unfolds, your communications requirements may change. Make sure all of your people have the resources they need to receive and act on orders as you issue them. If possible, establish dedicated frequencies for law enforcement responders and know the frequencies used by other agencies. You may need to pull people out in a hurry; you don't want to leave anyone behind because they didn't get the message.

There is one more ICS term we need to introduce here. Any actions you take at the scene management phase must be part of your overall Incident Action Plan (IAP). Your IAP should include both the tactics and the long-range strategies you will use to bring the incident under control. For example, if your primary consideration is removing barricaded gunmen from a school, your IAP must include details about the goal and the techniques you are going to use to achieve it (i.e., waiting them out, negotiating, or performing an assault).

You develop the IAP in conjunction with the other members of your unified command. This approach ensures the IAP meets the requirements of all participating agencies and/or disciplines. Make sure you receive input and analysis of the IAP from all main ICS functions.

Outcomes

Most incidents can be resolved at the scene management phase. Should that be the case, you would proceed to the "termination" phase. But, resolved or not, at the conclusion of the scene management phase you should at least have:

- Organized a decision-making team using ICS

- Developed an Incident Action Plan

- Established a unified command structure (if required)

There certainly are cases in which a situation can no longer be dealt with effectively by the on-scene command post. Once the above elements are in place, an incident can more easily migrate to the next level of management: the "executive management" phase.

Executive Management Phase

The children are out, but technicians have been unable to control the release of the hazardous material.

Hazmat responders determine that a larger area must be evacuated. The kill zone now includes a nursing home and the school to which the bus was headed. In addition to residents, you must now safely move 100 seniors and 250 elementary students.

Your evacuation area has spread into two other jurisdictions. Local and state officials as well as representatives from the local school district are responding to your command post. The large number of evacuees and the areas involved force you to recognize that you can no longer effectively manage the incident from the on-scene command post.

So how do you handle this escalation?

When the size, scope, and seriousness of an event exceed the capabilities of on-scene management, your incident has progressed to the "executive management" phase. This phase can last from several hours to several weeks or more.

These events are usually major incidents such as earthquakes, airline crashes, large-scale hazmat incidents, and civil disturbances. Remember that all critical incidents will move through the crisis phase. Most will make it to the scene management phase. You only transition to the executive management phase when a major event resolution requires a larger management team and the activation of an Emergency Operations Center (EOC).

Because this book focuses on scene management, our discussion of the executive management phase will be brief. As an incident supervisor, you should simply be aware that an additional level of response is available when a scene exceeds the ability of local resources to resolve it.

Initial Objectives and Strategies

The primary objective of the executive management phase is the establishment of the Emergency Operations Center. The EOC represents a fully expanded Incident Command System. An EOC can be set up off-site at a fixed location or be housed in a mobile response unit, which many larger jurisdictions maintain.

Perhaps the most critical step at this stage is identifying a new IC with overall command of the response. This individual could be a high-ranking member of the agency primarily responsible for the response, such as a police or fire chief, or your state emergency management director. Regardless, this individual has ultimate decision-making power, with the support and advice of other agency commanders.

As the scene commander, you will probably have input into the decision to escalate a response to the executive management phase. If you remain on the scene, you will now have a powerful resource to help coordinate your response. It's up to you to work effectively with a multi-disciplinary management group. It will be your responsibility to keep them informed of conditions in the field and give them the information they need to constantly review plans.

The Incident Action Plan is not a static document. The EOC must be flexible in its response to the latest field intelligence. If a modified evacuation plan becomes necessary, for example, you and your team can provide the information the EOC needs to formulate the plan.

When you need additional field resources, you should find the EOC has already ordered and deployed those resources to the staging area for your use. As you attempt to deal with an expanding crisis, you don't need to be trying to figure out where to get what you need. Let the EOC do it.

Keep the EOC honest. If it appears decisions are being made that do not correlate with your field observations, let them know. But be aware the EOC operates with the "big picture." It may well be that decisions that appear groundless to you may actually be sound. Don't be shy about asking for the logic behind the orders you receive. You also are a commander and have a right to be fully informed.

Outcomes

The executive management phase always results in termination. For better or worse, there is no higher level of critical incident management to which to escalate.

Termination Phase

As the vapor cloud dissipated and hazmat techs were able to contain liquids and drain the tanker, you maintained your perimeters. You made sure that all casualties were handled. With the threat controlled, you begin demobilizing resources and returning evacuees. Then you begin the assessment process.

Work with other departments to review your response. Check your time line and log to make sure you have all the information you're going to need to face the inquiries that inevitably follow any critical incident.

Can you document the information upon which you based your various decisions? Can you show that you acted reasonably?

And don't forget about the well-being of your people. This was a traumatic event. Are you prepared to respond to their emotional needs? Should you pay special attention to the first-responding officer that you ordered away from the scene and who had to leave the children on the bus?

These are just a few of the hard questions that will need to be answered. You're still under pressure, but the nature of your stress shifts from incident crisis to the microscope of hindsight review. Will you be prepared for it? Once the threat has been resolved, everybody gets to go home, right? Well, eventually. The termination phase frequently gets less attention than it merits. Many crucial tasks still need to be performed after an incident has been concluded.

Termination lasts as long as it lasts. It can take from a few hours to several weeks. The primary characteristic is the restoration of order and the return to normal operations for the public and all responding agencies. Demobilizing an extensive response can take time. You can't have people going back in-service by simply driving away from the scene of a critical incident.

Objectives and Strategies

Your first task during termination is to continue to ensure scene integrity. Most scenes require clean up and/or continued investigation. As first responders leave, new personnel, such as fire marshals or evidence techs, may need to perform duties at the scene.

This cannot be stressed enough. All too often we've seen perimeters collapse immediately following the resolution of an incident. After a gunman has been apprehended, for example. Officers working crowd control rush into the kill zone to offer support. This is when we find the media right in the middle of a scene interviewing traumatized victims and possibly destroying evidence. Give specific orders to maintain perimeters!

You need a plan for resuming normal operations. That includes accounting for all personnel, reporting injuries and damage, and reassigning responders to normal duties. Take your time. You now have the luxury of considered action.

You may have had the public evacuated from the kill zone. Provide for their orderly return to homes, schools, and businesses. This must be accomplished in a managed fashion. For example, before allowing residents to reoccupy evacuated homes in certain hazmat incidents, we must make sure pockets of gas have not become trapped in the homes. Hopefully you haven't released all of your fire or hazmat units with the appropriate detection equipment!

And not least of all: How are your people responding to the incident? Critical incident stress can undermine long-term health and operational efficiency. Make sure responders get the help they need to deal with exceptionally traumatic events. Depending on the severity of the incident, stress debriefings may be required for victims, bystanders, and responders. Your primary duty is to your people, but coordinate with other agencies to make sure all responders have access to the help and support they require.

How Did We Do?

Perhaps the most important task during the termination phase is your assessment of your response. There are three questions you should always ask:

- What happened?

- What was our response?

- What would we do differently next time?

Your report must clearly document the events that occurred and the actions you took. The log you initiate from the beginning of your response will be critical for your review of the incident management and any external professional or legal review that may be ordered. You will *not* be able to reconstruct events from memory.

A review of your response must be completely honest. Were your actions the best options? Did you clearly communicate your orders to subordinates? Did you fairly weigh observations and suggestions from subordinates or co-commanders in your unified command?

All critical incident evaluations bring up the same issue: Had we been aware of certain facts at the time, we might have made different decisions. It's the hindsight effect. But more often than not, based on the information we had at the time, we made what we believed to be correct decisions. We must bear in mind that, even when an incident did not go as planned, these decisions were *not* mistakes. They were simply decisions we made, based on the information we had at the time.

Don't be too hard on yourself. Remember that there are many factors that are out of our control. Did you focus on those you *could* control? Make careful note of the impediments to your response. We all face the same general issues. Did your radios function properly? Was crowd control effective? Did you encounter political opposition to your command?

And lastly, you are not alone in this analysis. You must assess the efforts and decisions of everyone in your command. When debriefing responders, perhaps the most confrontational question you can ask is, "what did you do wrong?" This immediately puts the responder on defensive. We suggest you ask, "what would you do different next time?" This is a less judgmental, more constructive way to approach your assessment.

Summary

We hope this chapter gave you a feel for the common stages and response strategies shared by all critical incidents. The phases discussed in this chapter would have been similar for a severe transport accident, a botched bank robbery turned hostage situation, or a tornado. It's just a question of type and scope. Regardless of the nature of the emergency, it's up to you as the supervisor to recognize the requirements for each phase and respond accordingly.

Review Questions

1. What are the characteristics of an incident in the crisis phase?

2. What are the primary goals of the first responding supervisor in the crisis phase?

3. What are two strategies for the first responding supervisor in the crisis phase?

4. What three questions should be asked during the assessment of an incident in the termination phase?

Three

Tactical Leadership

Objectives

After completing this chapter, you should be able to:

- *Identify the factors that determine leadership style*
- *Describe the value of tactical leadership in the crisis phase*
- *List the skills that must be mastered by the effective tactical leader*

As discussed in Chapter One, the focus of the supervisor responding to any critical incident must center on *controllable* factors. We have long subscribed to the theory that the *most* controllable factor in a critical incident is the individual supervisor. That's you.

There are as many different leadership styles as there are leaders. Successful styles vary according to the task: what works for a hospital administrator might not work for a shift manager at an auto-assembly plant. This chapter examines the consistent traits and style you need to successfully manage a critical incident in the early moments: the crisis phase.

But first you should recognize three common variables that affect management style. What we are talking about is situational leadership. Your style will vary dependent upon:

- **The subordinate.** Some people simply require more supervision than others. This affects the tasks you assign and the manner in which you manage personnel.

- **The supervisor.** How comfortable are you with a situation, your subordinates, or command in general?

- **The criticality of the task.** In a life-or-death situation, you and your subordinates will respond differently than if you were discussing a matter of policy. This is the primary factor that determines the management style needed at a critical incident. The more critical the task, the more directing you should be.

Of these three factors, which do *you* have the most control over? The task, your people, or you?

Leadership Style

If you are a police supervisor, ask yourself this simple question: "When is the last time I gave one of my subordinates a direct and specific order?" If you can't think of an instance, you're not alone. Giving orders in modern law enforcement has practically become a lost art. We have inundated our profession with trendy leadership styles from the private sector.

For years we have trained in the philosophies of democratic leadership, employee empowerment, and participatory management. The term "autocratic" tells us how *not* to supervise. The once simple act of giving orders has become uncomfortable for today's law enforcement supervisors. And as for *following* orders…!

This is not to disparage the more empowering leadership styles. Nor do we advocate their abandonment. They are valuable in most day-to-day contacts with our team. And they are appropriate when an event evolves into the scene management phase. However, they simply do not work when the supervisor is attempting to manage the early minutes (the crisis phase) of a critical incident.

Are You a Coach or a Player?

Law enforcement personnel (with the exception of specialists, such as SWAT) are the only emergency responders who arrive at the scene as individuals. It is only *at the scene* that we form into teams. Think of our counterparts in the fire service. Firefighters arrive on a rig together and each has specific assigned tasks. When did you last see several police officers pull up to an emergency scene in the same vehicle and immediately set about a series of predefined tasks?

Police departments expect initiative. We reward it. A common, positive note on employee performance reviews frequently reads something like "requires little supervision." In most cases, a police officer's independent style is necessary to do his or her job. In a critical incident, however, this characteristic is unacceptable. All responders must know the plan and stick to it. It's up to you to communicate the plan and make certain subordinates do exactly what they're told.

The police supervisor responds alone (usually) and creates his/her team from whatever resources are currently available. The supervisor assigns tasks and ensures the team interacts with other responders—all while the incident is unfolding. To accomplish this difficult task, the initial supervisor on an emergency scene must assume the non-politically correct "autocratic" style of leadership.

To lapse into sports analogy, you are the coach. You are not a player. A player does not have the big picture. A player performs a specific task assigned by the coach. You must step back from the action—no matter how hard it is!—and take in that big picture. Once you have assessed the situation and developed your game plan, you give your team the play.

A scene commander must issue specific and clear orders to responding units. That in itself may seem foreign; now add the stress of operating in some of the most tragic and horrific circumstances imaginable. It is imperative you demonstrate to responding personnel that you are in charge and have a clear plan to stabilize and ultimately resolve the crisis.

Crisis leadership forces you to make hard choices that must be respected by your subordinates. One of our students, for example, had to make a tough decision when an officer was shot during an incident. Because the gunman was still on the loose, the supervisor decided not to risk allowing other units into the area to care for the officer until the suspects, location, and potential kill zone could be better defined. He told us it was the toughest decision he has ever had to make—and not a popular one at the time. However, this is the type of informed decision that will save officers' lives.

Practice Makes Perfect

Practicing critical incident management is key. This applies to personal as well as tactical skills. A supervisor who waits until a critical incident to assume an autocratic persona will probably cause confusion among subordinates. "Who does this guy think he is? Why is he barking orders at me? He's never yelled at me before…" Without practice, you may not be able to implement a credible autocratic style of leadership.

Take advantage of opportunities to assume this leadership style. Use minor incidents, such as a non-injury MVA, to demonstrate to subordinates the dynamics you'll expect on a critical incident scene. Issue those clear and specific orders.

There are two primary points to keep in mind when you practice:

- You should discuss the sudden change with your subordinates first so they can anticipate your command style. Don't blind-side them with a drill-sergeant personality when all along you've been the nurturing type. Make sure subordinates understand how you expect them to comply with specific orders.

- Subsequently, you should assess your effectiveness as well as the response of your personnel to this style. Who followed orders and who didn't?

Through these situations, the supervisor can practice tactical leadership and the subordinate can practice tactical compliance. The better the "coach" and "player" understand their roles during the crisis phase, the more organized the initial response will be. Organization brings about a quicker, safer stabilization and resolution to the incident.

Now that we've identified the kind of supervision a critical incident requires, let's turn to the specific functions the supervisor must perform. Across the board, successful autocratic leaders do the following:

- Assess problems by taking in and evaluating data

- Decide on an appropriate course of action

- Clearly relate that course of action to others

- Maintain a command presence

Seem like common sense? You'd expect these traits from managers on a day-to-day basis, right? Perhaps, but the point is they are extremely difficult to carry out during the crisis phase of a critical incident. Now we'll take a closer look at each of these functions and how you can implement them successfully under stress.

Problem Assessment

Leadership in crisis requires the ability to take in data and process it under the most stressful conditions imaginable. You *must* do this, sometimes in a matter of seconds, or lives may be lost. The crisis phase of an incident is characterized by confusion, panic, rushing to the scene, and gridlock: All of these have a negative impact on information gathering.

In those critical first moments, you must ask the question: "What and/or whom am I dealing with?" You must also assess the risk to your personnel. Although this is a common practice in both fire and EMS training, it is seldom talked about in police training. The bottom line: a dead officer can't help anyone. Of course we perform unsafe acts. That's practically a definition of law enforcement! A proper risk assessment, however, ensures we perform them as safely as possible.

Quick assessment of the scope of the emergency and the risks posed by it can make all the difference between stabilizing a scene or allowing it to spiral out of control. Later we will discuss specific strategies you can use in this process. For now we will focus on the skill of problem assessment as a whole.

Individuals with good problem assessment skills seldom overestimate or underestimate the seriousness of a situation. Two of the most common and inappropriate approaches a supervisor can take are:

- The "Chicken Little" approach, where every call is a critical incident.

- The "One Riot, One Ranger" approach, where no call is a critical incident.

Each misguided approach shares the same flaw: prejudging an incident. Instead, manage each incident on its own merits according to the information you have. Law enforcement is in a unique position here; if we don't do it, nobody will. We're often the first ones on the scene. Fire and EMS services train their personnel to use one simple risk assessment technique: Call the *cops* to find out if certain scenes are safe!

In one sense, managing critical incidents is similar to every call you respond to. Prejudging a call before arriving and assessing the scene can get you into serious trouble. Surely you can think of examples of poor problem assessment skills you have encountered in *other* supervisors. When poor assessment does not result in death or injury, mishandled events can become popular history and an opportunity for ribbing. Unfortunately, poor problem assessment skills can also cost officers and the public their lives.

To obtain information in a crisis, tactical leaders exploit any and all available resources. These sources may not be "official." A hazmat technician, for example, may not be on-scene or available during the crisis phase of a tanker spill. Good leaders use who or what may be available at the time. If one of your on-duty officers has a specialized skill area such as SWAT, volunteer fire, or hazmat, use that person's knowledge to perform the problem assessment. Keep that person by you as you handle a scene in their area of familiarity. Remember the old saying: "Good supervisors don't need to know all the answers, just where to find them."

And the time to look for those sources is not during a crisis. To the best of your ability, try to familiarize yourself with the special skills your officers can bring to a scene *before* you need them.

Decision Making

Good problem assessment skills make for good information and thus result in good decisions. After a quick assessment of the situation at hand, the crisis leader must decide on a course of action to stabilize the scene. As basic as this strategy sounds, it is not uncommon for supervisors to be so caught up in collecting information that they fail to make some basic decisions. You can *never* get all the information. You must act on what you have.

Back to sports. Think of the quarterback who is unable to decide on a receiver when under pressure. The inability to select a course of action usually results in an interception, sack, or incomplete pass.

Top quarterbacks make snap decisions and then follow through. They make the decision to throw based on the information they have at the time. Yet even the best get intercepted. The same holds true for scene commanders. You make decisions based on what you know. You simply cannot wait for all the information.

Three things can cause a supervisor's inaction:

- stress overload
- personal indecisiveness
- organizational culture

Whereas overload and indecisiveness are individual issues, organizational culture is not. It is something you can change through awareness and training.

As you will read repeatedly in these pages, it is imperative in crisis management to force decision making to the *lowest possible level*. The immediate need to stabilize a situation transcends any formal chain of command or daily standard operating procedure. Minutes of inaction during the crisis phase can translate into additional property damage, personal injuries, or loss of life.

We have mentioned the need for a "game plan" to address incidents. Well, if a sergeant has been rebuked or second-guessed for incident response decisions one too many times, her "game plan" when responding to an incident will be...to call the lieutenant! And if that lieutenant has been burned, his "game plan" will be...you can imagine.

The first-responding supervisor cannot be reduced to inaction while waiting for a higher-level commander. That first supervisor must take immediate responsibility and assume command of the scene. This requires rapid decision-making. A supervisor concerned with any priority beyond containment and control (such as politics) will not be decisive and will not take command.

Issuing Orders and Directions

Some say issuing orders and directions is a skill. Some say it's an art. The method you use to relate plans and strategies to others depends on your personal style. You have a lot of orders to issue, and success results when your team accomplishes all the little things correctly. Disaster can result when lots of little balls get dropped due to miscommunication.

Have you ever given an order or direction to a subordinate and then had that individual do something totally different? In these cases we usually fault the subordinate. In fact, one of two things actually happened. Either the receiver *did* misunderstand the order or they did *exactly* what we communicated to them. This is a clear, but subtle distinction: they didn't do what we wanted them to do; they did what we told them to do.

The ability to develop a picture in your mind and then relate it to others is not as easy as it sounds. This is especially difficult when the receiver is not present and we cannot supplement our words with gestures, illustrations, and other visual aids.

In the overwhelming majority of critical incidents, we give orders and directions to responding units via the radio. As discussed earlier, our radios introduce a number of inherent communication obstacles. Remember, the lowest bidder has produced most of your equipment. At times that's exactly the way it performs! However, let's assume your equipment is functioning correctly. Now the burden is squarely on you to communicate orders clearly and concisely. No excuses: it's just you, your radio, and your subordinates.

During a barricaded gunman incident you give an order to seal off an intersection. You get on the radio and say: "Car 302. Proceed to the intersection of Main and Second and block traffic." What haven't you said?

- How can the officer get to the location safely? Do they know where your kill zone is?

- What specifically is expected of them when they arrive there? Should they stop traffic in all directions?

You must anticipate and answer these questions in the orders you give. You know what you want. Does your subordinate? Therefore, the more appropriate order might be: "Proceed to the intersection of Main and Second. Approach from the South on Main and prevent traffic from proceeding northbound on Main from Second." If this is what you are envisioning, this is what must be related to your responders.

If there is any doubt as to whether your subordinate got the message, have them repeat to you what they will do based on your orders and directions. The ability to clearly communicate with other responders in a critical incident is essential to implementing any plan or operational tactic.

Think you can do that without practice?

Command Presence

This is, perhaps, the quintessential "you-know-it-when-you-see-it" leadership trait. Simply put, a crisis leader with command presence communicates confidence and control to subordinates through his or her actions. The mere tone of the supervisor's voice over the radio can incite anxiety or calm a situation. The ability to minimize confusion and panic in the initial minutes of a critical incident is essential to stabilization.

In the canine corps there is a saying that "everything goes down lead." Translated, the dog becomes the handler. If the handler is excited, the dog will become excited. If the handler has a laid-back attitude, the dog will assume *that* trait. If you are fortunate enough to work with these teams, check this out the next time you call for canine assistance. You'll be amazed how true it is.

In management, this concept means your subordinates take on your attitudes and characteristics. The hard-charging, aggressive units are usually headed by supervisors possessing these characteristics. In crisis management, this means your subordinates will mirror your controlled and confident response.

How do you achieve this presence? To some it comes naturally. For others it requires practice. One common technique is simply taking a moment to calm yourself before giving orders. This is very similar to the emotional gathering we perform before transmitting during a pursuit. Using this technique, an officer may be experiencing all of the adrenal-fed physical reactions (accelerated heart beat, time distortion, etc.), but still sound as if he were ordering breakfast at the local diner.

A supervisor must bring adrenalin reactions under control before giving orders, whether in person or on the radio. When you are overexcited, your communication is usually garbled and stresses your responders. Experienced officers force themselves to be clear and concise. A good crisis leader must be able to do the same. The ability to direct others in a calm, professional manner when the entire world seems to be coming apart is usually described as "command presence under fire." Command presence in a critical incident communicates confidence and control to your subordinates. They in turn will respond confidently and with control.

Civil Liability

One final point needs to be made about leadership and decision-making. You will find this book does not dwell much on civil liability. Frankly, as long as law enforcement does its job in a manner professional and consistent with SOPs, it is not an overwhelming concern. Critical incident management, however, is one major exception. If an event is major and controversial, you *will* come under a mountain of scrutiny once it is resolved. And you can certainly be the target of a civil suit if it appears your actions were unwarranted. But the news isn't all bad.

As a supervisor, you should realize there exists a fairly consistent standard for determining the appropriateness of your actions in any critical incident. That standard states, in substance: "Based upon the information available at the time a decision was made, did the supervisor act as a reasonable person would have?"

Note that the standard does not allow the reviewing body—be it a federal court, civilian review panel, or other inquiry—to consider information learned *subsequent* to the moment of the decision. This greatly limits "second guessing" decisions made in the heat of crisis.

This standard has probably been applied during the review of incidents in which you have been involved. But remember, you must be able to prove what you knew and when you knew it. Your incident log is critical!

Summary

Analysis of hundreds of critical incidents has shown the traits discussed in this chapter are mandatory for leaders in critical incidents. Failure to master skills in these areas will almost certainly have a direct negative impact on your ability to stabilize and resolve an incident in the crisis phase.

Remember, *you* are the most controllable factor on your scene. When you have yourself in hand, your subordinates will better fall into line. After that, all you have to do is manage the incident!

Review Questions

1. What are three factors that can determine management style?

2. How are team members and the public likely to respond to tactical leadership in the crisis phase?

3. How can you hone your tactical command presence?

4. List four skills that must be mastered by the effective tactical leader.

Four

Seven Critical Tasks

Objectives

After completing this chapter, you should be able to:

- *State the value of a "universal game plan" for crisis phase response*

- *Establish a control-oriented response to the crisis phase*

- *Describe each of the Seven Critical Tasks*

- *Identify resources you can bring to bear on a critical incident*

The first moments of an incident's development are crucial. This is where you control the situation or it controls you. You *can* contain a scene in the early stages and make decisions that will help ensure long-term resolution. But to do so, you must take actions we refer to as *critical tasks*.

The decisions you make to accomplish the tasks will vary depending upon the specifics of the incident you are attempting to stabilize. As this text has emphasized, similar problems or obstacles exist in the crisis phase of almost every critical incident. Experience shows us, therefore, that a game plan that minimizes their negative impact will apply in all situations, regardless of the type of incident or the location where it occurs.

The critical tasks in this chapter give you that universal game plan.

This approach to the early phases of critical incidents differs markedly from both the training you may have received in the academy and the actions you take daily when responding to calls. The emphasis in the crisis phase must be on stabilization, *not* resolution. If you look too far into the future, events developing in the present may spiral out of control. We refer to this as "tunnel vision." It leads to all kinds of problems.

The Seven Critical Tasks are:

1. Establish control and communications

2. Identify the kill zone

3. Establish the inner perimeter

4. Establish the outer perimeter

5. Establish the on-scene command post

6. Establish a staging area

7. Identify and request additional resources

Although we present the tasks in this sequence, you should not consider them a "one-two-three" solution. Instead, think of the critical tasks as pieces of a puzzle. Accomplish all of the tasks, regardless of order of completion, and you will enhance your chances of success. Omit any specific task and you make your job of containment and stabilization much more difficult.

These critical tasks have been validated by the thousands of police supervisors and other responders we have trained since 1990. If you ever need to use them, we'd like to hear about *your* experience.

1. Establish Control and Communications

Assuming control of an incident means more than just driving up on-scene. We frequently hear supervisors say: "If I go, people know I'm in charge." This cavalier attitude simply doesn't work when new officers aren't familiar with your voice or there are multiple agencies responding. Announce your command both at the scene and to dispatch.

Our counterparts in the fire service are unambiguous about command assumption. "Engine 132 will be Main Street command." We hear this all the time. Why is it so difficult for police supervisors to do the same?

Frequently, the responding law enforcement supervisor may be the only supervisor on duty for that shift. They may consider announcements of command to be pompous or egotistical. *They are not!* Announcing your response to and command of the scene removes any question as to who is in charge. On-scene personnel know to whom they should direct their requests, questions, and information. Dispatch knows to whom it should direct external communications.

For example, a first-responding supervisor with call number "Car 20" would issue a brief and simple radio transmission, such as: "Car 20 to Dispatch. I am responding to 250 Main Street. I'll be assuming command of the scene. Keep all units responding to the incident on this frequency and take all other traffic to a secondary frequency." If no secondary frequency is available then give the order to hold all non-emergency communications. We'll discuss frequencies in more detail shortly.

Problem Assessment

Once you've assumed control of the scene, your next step is to size up the situation. Good sources of information include initial responders and bystanders, if they are available. Ask initial responders the following questions:

- What is the nature of the incident?

- What is the exact location of the incident?

- How many suspects am I dealing with?

- What is the number and type of weapons involved?

- What type of chemical is involved?

- Is this a possible terrorist threat?

As basic as this sounds, determining the exact nature and location of the threat may be one of the most difficult tasks you must perform in the crisis phase of an incident. This task is further complicated by the confusion that characterizes the crisis phase of an incident. Determining the exact location of an incident is an early priority. As you seek this information, bear in mind that the severity of the incident and resultant stress factors, such as the number of dead or injured, has a direct impact on the communication abilities of those reporting to and those involved in the incident.

For example, a commercial airline crash in San Diego, California, showed that a downed commercial airliner in a highly populated area could be difficult to pinpoint. During the crisis phase, dispatch sent units to both Falcon Street and similar-sounding Felton Street—even though the streets were several blocks apart. In this case, the sheer magnitude of the incident crippled the ability of both dispatch and responders to communicate clearly.

To pinpoint the exact location of an incident, you may need to calm both communications personnel and/or first units on the scene. Maintain your composure and others will do the same.

You must also remain calm in the face of different *kinds* of threats. For example, most law enforcement personnel recognize gunfire as life threatening. Therefore, it tends to restrain officers from taking unsafe actions at a scene. Unfortunately, that same cannot be said for chemical releases, whether accidental or intentional.

Depending on the nature of the threat, your hardest decision may be to do…nothing. Stories of police officers being seriously injured or killed in chemical releases are all too common. When you see an officer down, your first instinct is to rush to assist. We go in. That's what we do! But in hazmat situations, as we'll discuss later, the fire services usually have the appropriate tools and the primary scene responsibility. Your job may be to restrain your own resources from charging in and becoming part of the problem.

Communications

In any crisis situation, establishing communications must be a priority. You are going to need to talk to possibly dozens of people to obtain and share intelligence about the incident. You must make sure the communication lines are open and that they stay open.

As law enforcement supervisors, we have become conditioned to keeping the main frequency available for normal traffic and therefore usually take any unusual occurrence to a secondary frequency. In the crisis phase of a critical incident we must break this habit. During the crisis phase, keep your radio communications on the original frequency used when the incident began. Tell dispatch to send all other traffic to a secondary frequency, if available.

This simple but critical act not only clarifies lines of communications but also informs communications personnel that a supervisor is assuming command of the scene. Any attempt to change the main communication format only enhances the possibility of communications failures.

If you have access to alternate radio frequencies, use them later in the scene management phase when you have more time and resources. If you are working with one frequency, restrict traffic to incident-specific communications as much as possible.

When using phone lines, make sure they stay open and available. Don't rely on cell phones: everyone even remotely associated with the incident will be trying to make calls and cell relays will become overloaded. Try to get dedicated landlines.

You may need runners. You may need hand signals! Regardless of the communication mode, secure it so you'll always have access to it.

Of course, communications extend beyond the incident scene. If you cannot control the situation in the early phases, you may also need to establish lines to an extended ICS team operating remotely. Make sure you have the landlines, cellular, or radio capacity to work with remote groups. Generally, this level of communication is a characteristic of the scene management phase.

2. Identify the Kill Zone

"Kill zone" is a harsh but descriptive term for the area immediately surrounding an incident—the area of imminent danger to responders and citizens. This is the field of fire for gunmen barricaded in a house. This is the location of a ruptured tanker and the cloud path of the chlorine gas leaking from it.

Why "kill zone?" Why not something less intimidating and more politically correct? There's a good reason. Calling it the "danger zone" doesn't work because then every responding officer would run right into it. They *do* danger! The same goes for calling it the "hot zone." Every firefighter would be in there. They do *hot*! We need a term that clearly describes what would happen if you or a member of the public were to enter. You could be killed. That tends to get everyone's attention—even cops'.

Figure 4-1 on the next page shows a potential kill zone for a barricaded gunman with a small-caliber handgun in the first floor apartment at 250 Main Street. In this case, the kill zone is the suspect's field of fire as limited by nearby buildings.

In this scenario, the correct initial radio transmission by the supervisor would sound something like this: "All cars responding to the incident at 250 Main Street. **I want *no* cars on Main Street between Second avenue and Third avenue.**" This simple transmission identifies the kill zone to all responding units, prevents inadvertent response into the area, and may well save officers' lives. The kill zone may be as small as a portion of a city block, as depicted in Figure 4-1, or may involve multiple city blocks or entire towns, in the case of a chemical spill or civil disorder.

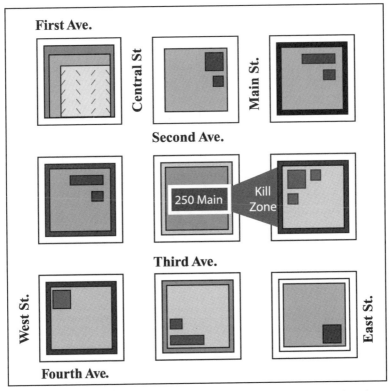

Figure 4-1: The shaded area shows the kill zone for a barricaded gunman in a first floor apartment with a small-caliber handgun. The kill zone represents the suspect's field of fire.

Critical incidents can happen anywhere. For an incident on an interstate highway, responders may define the kill zone on the radio like this: "No cars on Interstate 90 between mile marker 128 and mile marker 129." The physical identification of the kill zone will vary from incident to incident, but the need to clearly identify that area will not.

Once you've identified this zone, deploy personnel to ensure no one moves in or out of the area (public *and* responders). The two exceptions are evacuations and controlled movement. And as we'll see later when we get into more on hazardous materials responses, it can frequently make more sense for civilians to shelter-in-place. On a windy day, a hazmat kill zone can be deceptively large, making an evacuation impractical.

Controlled movement refers to getting the public clear of the kill zone. You do not, however, simply let them run screaming into the surrounding neighborhood. Chances are you might lose suspects and witnesses that way. If you have any reason to believe suspects may try to mingle with the crowd, pat down and interview all persons leaving a criminal scene. At a minimum, take names and check IDs. You may need these people later.

As Figure 4-2 shows, the kill zones for a barricaded gunman and a hazmat spill would be very different. The first is determined by the caliber of the gunman's weapon and the surrounding buildings. The second is determined by the size and nature of the spill and then by wind and terrain.

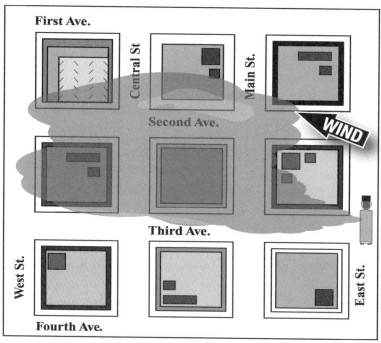

Figure 4-2: Numerous factors—such as wind, terrain, and the nature of the release—can affect a hazmat kill zone.

There are no hard and fast rules for the size of a kill zone. Your own observations of the terrain, the surrounding buildings, the nature of the threat, and weather conditions will dictate how large it will be. For some situations, such as a hazmat incident, the kill zone can expand rapidly, forcing you to be extra conservative in your threat estimates.

The size and shape of the kill zone determines the size and shape of our next critical task: the inner perimeter.

3. Establish the Inner Perimeter

The inner perimeter defines the area just beyond the kill zone and within which responders operate to directly control the situation. One of your primary jobs is to strictly limit inner perimeter access to responding emergency agencies.

The inner perimeter is *not the kill zone*. It's the line immediately behind which you and other responders are working. The boundary of the inner perimeter must completely surround the kill zone and be tightly controlled to keep the incident from expanding. You control access to the kill zone, directing who goes in (such as a coordinated assault team) and who goes out (such as fleeing suspects trying to blend in with a crowd). This is the boundary beyond which you conduct all operations. Although the inner perimeter can be an offensive position, it must afford cover, concealment, and/or proper safe distance for responders working behind it.

Remember, your objective at this point is containment. The boundary must be stable and your people should have assigned posts that they do not leave. *No independent actions* should be taken: This is one of those times when personnel should do only what you tell them to do. Independent action from an inner perimeter position can make things worse. By nature, officers constantly reevaluate and try to improve their strategic locations. This usually translates to getting closer to the scene. Left uncontrolled, this tendency has on numerous occasions led to officers exposing themselves unnecessarily to gunfire within the kill zone and further complicated an already deadly situation.

Figure 4-3 shows a typical inner perimeter set up in response to the barricaded gunman at 250 Main Street. The next several paragraphs will refer to this illustration.

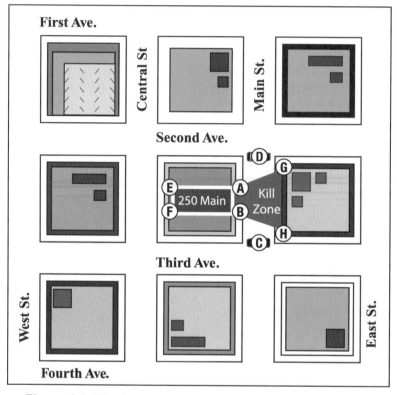

Figure 4-3: The inner perimeter defines the boundary within which responders work to contain and resolve the incident. This illustration shows a possible inner perimeter for a barricaded gunman with a small-caliber weapon.

A and **B** represent the first responding officers. They answered the initial call and got pinned down by gunfire at the scene. You, as the first responding supervisor, have announced response to and command of the scene. You conducted a brief problem assessment, identified the kill zone, and communicated that information to additional responding units. Although this zone may change as the situation evolves, such as suspects opening up with longer-range weapons or gaining access to higher ground, the area posing the known danger to first responders has been identified.

You must now deploy resources to contain and control the situation. Marked units **C** and **D** are positioned to block off all vehicular and pedestrian traffic from entering the area. This includes emergency vehicles and personnel responding to the scene.

You must deploy resources with clear and concise radio communications. Orders must contain not only duties, but also the route for safe arrival at the desired location. You may be the only one who has this information. Share it! For example, a command given to marked unit **C** might sound something like this: "Respond to the intersection of Main Street and Third Avenue. Avoid Main Street between Second and Third. Approach the intersection from the South on Main or the West on Third. Stop all vehicular and pedestrian traffic from proceeding Northbound on Main Street."

A similar direction—complete with safe access route and duties upon arriving—would be given to marked unit **D**. These types of detailed communications may seem cumbersome, but they are exactly what the phrase *clear, concise order giving* means. Don't assume your people know something that you take for granted. Keep it brief, but spell it out.

Positions **E**, **F**, **G** and **H** represent other officers that may be deployed in safe cover around the incident scene to ensure containment. As you would expect, their orders should also include safe routes and detailed directions as to their duties and responsibilities. These positions may be temporary. Specially trained personnel, such as SWAT, may relieve most, if not all, of their positions.

Some supervisors might attempt to remove officers **A** and **B** from the kill zone immediately. That may be a good strategy if it can be accomplished safely and without compromising the containment of the suspect. However, it may be impossible to achieve without undue risk. Also, officers pinned down may refuse to move for fear of exposure. If you decide to attempt an extraction, make sure you take the affected officers' input into account! The procedure will require their cooperation. If the officers have adequate cover and are in a position of relative safety, they should be left in place until they can be moved safely with the assistance of specialized personnel and equipment.

A few other points need to be made about the inner perimeter. As just stated, the inner perimeter must afford cover, concealment and/or proper safe distance for responders working behind it. Good cover is usually defined as the position we put ourselves in immediately *after* the first shot is fired in our direction. Your job as supervisor is to make sure responders have proper cover *before* they draw the attention of a gunman.

Assess the cover requirements of the assigned units before sending them into harm's way. Keep in mind that this is extremely difficult to do if you have positioned yourself as a player instead of a coach.

As an active participant, you can develop a narrow perspective that severely limits your ability to see the big picture. Place yourself in a position that allows you to conduct ongoing assessments of the scene (and all of its elements) in relative safety. You can't do that if you're crouching behind a trash bin to avoid hostile fire. Of course it's possible you may start out as a player at a scene, but pull back as soon as you can. We know you would probably rather be right in there on the front lines. Don't worry about what anyone might think! You have multiple responsibilities, and cover assessment is just one of them.

Of course, cover from a gunman is not the same as cover from a cloud of poisonous gas. When faced with a ruptured chlorine tanker, for example, your people need to be a minimum of 900 feet away and upwind. This figure comes not from a visual assessment of the scene and your own street smarts, but from an invaluable reference book, the *USDOT Emergency Response Guidebook*. We go into the ERG in more detail in Appendix B (see page 175).

The inner perimeter may not be as dangerous as the kill zone, but it still requires significant safety measures. Cover in the case of hazmat means either distance from a scene or protective clothing, which your responders won't have. Therefore, they must rely on training and experience to avoid contact with a released substance.

Our next two points pertain to people within the inner perimeter. The first concerns plainclothes personnel. It may seem obvious to limit inner perimeter access to emergency responders. Now we'll take that a step farther and argue that, particularly in criminal scenes, responders should be limited to *uniformed* personnel. If plainclothes are initially deployed, remove them and replace them with uniforms as soon as possible. The wide success of plainclothes units has been due in part to their ability to blend into the general population. They are indistinguishable. You don't want to put your detectives at undue risk from members of other departments or overzealous homeowners.

Of course, removing plainclothes personnel from an inner perimeter isn't always an option. If the only officers available to contain a suspect are plainclothes personnel, then use them. However, you as the supervisor must make their presence *very clear* to all responding units. Use positions and descriptions, if necessary. Failure to do so may have tragic results.

The second point deals with the general public. During the crisis phase of a critical incident there may well be innocent people trapped within the inner perimeter also. In the scenario depicted in Figure 4-3, the areas identified as the kill zone and the inner perimeter could contain numerous civilians.

Usually, the best strategy in the crisis phase is to keep individuals who are in relatively safe locations, such as their homes, in those locations until they can be moved in a safe and orderly manner. This strategy is known as *shelter-in-place*. It is a strategy often used in chemical spills that involve no threat of fire or explosion (see page 138).

The alternative to shelter-in-place is *evacuation*. However, evacuation is seldom a good option in the crisis phase of an incident. Evacuation is almost always better accomplished in the scene management phase when sufficient resources are available to carry out this tactic.

Although crisis containment and responder safety are paramount, you should not let the public be an afterthought. As part of the problem assessment process during the crisis phase, determine who or what might be endangered within the perimeters you've established. Accept that you may not be able to adequately handle the public as well as you might like at this point. That may have to wait until the scene management phase.

Lastly, take areas of critical vulnerability into account when you create your inner perimeter. Such areas can include hospitals, schools, gun shops, and power plants. Anything that could significantly add to the seriousness of the incident if it were to become involved must be locked down as quickly as possible. For example, if you don't want your hostage situation to involve a nearby school, it's up to you to recognize the threat and make sure the building is locked down or evacuated, depending on the specific situation.

The bottom line is that during the crisis phase you must identify and secure the public and at-risk locations to the best of your ability. That gives you the breathing room you need to develop and implement more detailed response strategies in the scene management phase.

4. Establish the Outer Perimeter

While the inner perimeter controls the incident, the outer perimeter controls the *response* to the incident. You will have crowds. Specifically, three types of crowds:

- Civilian bystanders, which vary by location and time of day

- The media, which vary by location as well as the nature and severity of the incident

• Emergency responders, which also vary with the type of incident

(Prepare, however, for a major media and emergency response even in remote areas with small civilian populations.)

The area between the inner and outer perimeters is where responders get their work done. It is essential that you tightly control access to this area. Even other responders can cause confusion if they have unrestrained access to a scene. The appropriate deployment of arriving units is one of your essential scene command tasks. That frequently means establishing a staging area, an area to which resources can respond and from which you can deploy them as required. (We will discuss staging later in this chapter; see page 76.)

The typical management problem transitions from too few resources in the crisis phase to possibly too many resources in the scene management phase. Those large numbers of resources require careful management to make sure they are used to their maximum efficiency.

Time and again the initial response of emergency responders to a scene has caused gridlock and inhibited successful operations. This forces you to disconnect from scene management and concentrate on undoing the gridlock. Valuable time and energy is focused on a problem *caused* by those who are attempting to help. The early establishment of an outer perimeter provides an open area in which to stage and operate and an additional safety zone for non-emergency workers.

Figure 4-4 depicts with police units a typical outer perimeter responders might establish for the 250 Main Street gunman incident. The outer perimeter has been established far enough away from the incident location to guarantee public safety outside its limits, yet close enough to keep the area between the inner and outer perimeters a manageable size.

The outer perimeter is not an offensive position. If it becomes so, then it's too close to the actual incident. Its primary function is to control movement to and from the scene, not deal directly with developments in the kill zone. As with the inner perimeter, personnel assigned to outer perimeter posts should be sent to specific locations and instructed to stay there.

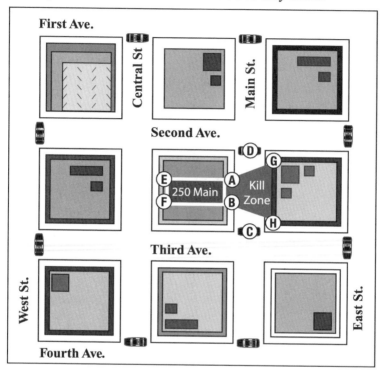

Figure 4-4: The outer perimeter (represented by the black and white units on the outside edge of the illustration) for a barricaded gunman. The region between the inner and outer perimeters provides a safe work area for responders.

A good field test to apply to an outer perimeter is whether non-police personnel can staff it safely. If you feel the need for armed officers on your outer perimeter, then you have not positioned the boundary correctly. No weapons should be unholstered or displayed at any point on the outer perimeter. The inner perimeter is the business end; *that's* where your offensive resources should be deployed.

The mere presence and readiness of firearms on the outer perimeter opens the door to inappropriate response. Officers beyond effective range might fire toward a central location surrounded by other responders. Your job is to minimize this possibility by making sure there are no weapons at the ready position on the outer perimeter. Unless there is potential for serious civil unrest, officers at outer stations need be armed only with the tools essential for traffic and crowd control. They need also be aware of relevant incident information that they can pass on to responding units, such as command post and staging area locations.

To be effective, the outer perimeter must completely enclose the inner perimeter. The actual size of the perimeter depends entirely on the scale and nature of the event. For example, if you expect four entire fire companies and two hazmat response teams on-scene, your outer boundary had better expand to allow for those vehicles to stage securely.

The outer perimeter example we've used so far has been based on criminal activity. But recall the cloud of chlorine gas in Figure 4-2. With a variable kill zone comes a variable inner perimeter and a variable outer perimeter. In this case, where are you going to be comfortable allowing crowds to gather? Depending on weather conditions, you may be looking at an outer perimeter of possibly dozens of city blocks. Play it safe!

When a rail tanker explosion demolished 90% of the business district of Crescent City, Illinois, there were no fatalities. Responders recognized the threat in time and evacuated the entire town. The lesson? Even your inner perimeter can quickly look like the borders of a mid-sized township. It's unlikely you would have the resources to completely enclose an area that size with an outer perimeter. In that case, you would simply blockade incoming traffic and set up a working area on one edge of the evacuated area. It would be big enough to hold staging and command functions, but small enough for you to control access.

Now that you have established the incident scene layout and created a place to work, it's time to turn to the tasks you must accomplish to coordinate your resources. The final three critical tasks also happen to be important components of the Incident Command System and, by extension, the National Incident Management System.

5. Establish the On-Scene Command Post

At just about any scene, the supervisor's vehicle will serve as the initial command post. Therefore, where you park your vehicle upon arriving on-scene is critical to your ability to command the incident. The mere location selected may make the difference in whether you will be a participant/player or a manager/coach.

Any command post, whether it's a mobile or fixed site, must be located outside of the kill zone and between the inner and outer perimeters. This gives your people (and you!) safe access to the command post in a controlled area. The initial placement of your vehicle should also meet these criteria: not so close that you come under threat, and not so far away that you'll have to move closer once you establish the outer perimeter.

This assumes that other responders get to the scene before you. This may not always be the case. If you are one of the initial responders to arrive on-scene, you may choose to position your vehicle to deny access to the kill zone. In this case you stay there until you can get another unit to replace you. Only then can you back off the front line to a safe and controlled location.

As discussed earlier, if you remain on the inner perimeter your focus will be on event particulars and not on the overall operation. Only by removing yourself from the immediacy of the action can you develop that broad overview of the situation you need to be an effective supervisor. There is a common management principle that tells us we tend to manage what we can see. If we put ourselves on the inner perimeter of an incident, we will tend to manage from that perspective and possibly fail to handle issues not in our immediate line of sight.

*Any command post, either fixed or mobile, should **not** be located within line of sight of an incident, especially those involving armed individuals.*

If you can see them, they can see you. The last thing you want to give suspects is a bird's eye view of the activities at your command post. By locating a command post out of sight of an incident, you not only enhance the security and safety of command post personnel, but you also force the management of the scene to a different perspective. And what is that perspective? The big picture.

Figure 4-5 indicates one possible location for the initial supervisor to park his or her vehicle for our gunman scenario. This spot would also be a good choice for the establishment of a fixed-site command post. Keep in mind this is only one of several potential sites.

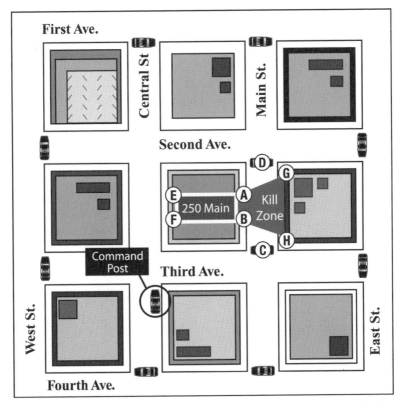

Figure 4-5: A command post should be in a safe, controlled location. This illustration shows the first responding supervisor's unit within the outer perimeter and beyond the line of sight of the kill zone.

We know now our command post should not be in or near the kill zone because of line-of-sight and command perspective issues. But there's another factor to consider: wind direction. While we always take wind into account during chemical or hazardous material incidents, we tend to neglect it when addressing barricaded or armed suspects. That is, until the deployment of tear gas by a SWAT team incapacitates our command post, which we have located downwind from an incident. Employing chemical weapons to extricate or temporarily incapacitate armed suspects is standard operating procedure for SWAT teams. You can't manage a scene if you're suffering as much as your suspects.

Wind direction may not be a major factor in the initial placement of the supervisor's vehicle. This is by definition a *mobile* command post. As the initial supervisor, you may park your vehicle only to then realize you are downwind from the suspect location. You move. However, wind must definitely be considered when you select a fixed-site location.

As the incident progresses, any number of variables (weather, requirements of your responding resource, length of operation, etc.) may require additional changes of location. It is your responsibility as the first responding supervisor to identify a safe and appropriate command post location. Whether the location remains static for the entire incident is immaterial. It may well change. You should not feel that your authority or decision-making ability is being questioned.

Few critical incidents can be stabilized and resolved using only a police vehicle as a command post. Two more likely alternatives are a transfer of authority to a fixed-site or to a mobile command post vehicle. Of course, the location of either should meet the same criteria outlined for the initial placement of the supervisor's vehicle.

Fixed-Site Command Post

The transition from a single-vehicle command post to a fixed site command post usually occurs when your requested resources arrive at the emergency scene. These resources may be additional supervisory law enforcement personnel, fire personnel, emergency medical service personnel, or specialists requested for scene resolution. If you do not have ready access to a mobile command vehicle, establish a fixed site location.

To be effective, your fixed command post must have the following:

- Electricity

- Drinking water

- Restroom facilities

- Access to telephone lines

- Ability to monitor television broadcasts

Remember, although cellular phones may be of great assistance in the crisis phase and early on in the scene management, you still need telephone landlines. Cellular systems are prone to overload and are less secure even than the radio frequencies we use daily.

The command post should have heat in the winter and air conditioning in the summer. If such options are unavailable, the command post should at least provide shelter from the elements and an atmosphere conducive to communication and decision-making processes. Avoid open-air command posts. Even if weather is not a factor, the noise and activity of an open-air command post can be a major distraction.

The availability of television and video equipment, once thought a luxury, is now a necessity. This equipment may well provide intelligence that can be vital to decision making. The same can be said of computers, fax machines, copiers, and other equipment that has become part of our daily administrative lives. Chances are if you find yourself setting up a fixed site location, the incident may last for quite a while. Make sure the command post supports the command functions and provides for all conceivable needs.

Mobile Command Post Vehicles

The other likely option is to transition to a mobile command post vehicle. Mobile command posts can, by nature, be redeployed easily. For example, a mobile command post is always preferable in a hazardous material incident due to the possibility of wind change and the subsequent need to fall back to a safer area.

All of the elements required for a fixed site should be available in a mobile command post. In the last several years numerous companies have begun producing vehicles that meet these requirements. Such vehicles, we feel, are truly worth the investment.

Unfortunately, jurisdictions frequently misuse mobile command posts as nothing more than mobile communications centers. Filled with additional radios, telephones, and assorted other equipment, they often lack the critical, basic requirements of an adequate command post. If in fact the mobile command post available to you is nothing more than a communication vehicle, use it in conjunction with a fixed site.

Regardless of which option you choose, there is always one common requirement for any adequate command post: It must provide an atmosphere conducive to the communication and decision-making processes that will take place. The command post must have the ability to minimize stress factors, such as noise, confusion, and panic, and the distracting effects they can have on those in charge.

6. Establish a Staging Area

The staging area is a specific location to which additional resources respond and await deployment to the scene. Do not confuse the staging area and the command post. These two terms have often been interchanged and many times the two functions end up as a combined area. Keep them separate, if possible.

In smaller incidents, such as a minor chemical spill, it *may* be appropriate to combine command and staging. However, in a barricaded gunman or armed hostage situation, the two should always be separate. Combined command post/staging areas tend to be crowded, difficult to access, and noisy. This does not make for the calm, quiet decision-making atmosphere we look for in a proper command post!

The area designated for staging should be well out of the kill zone, but between the inner and outer perimeters. It must be large enough to accommodate all of the responding resources, and close enough to allow for quick transfer to and from the scene. Parking lots and blocked off streets are optimum locations. Figure 4-6 gives a possible location for our incident at 250 Main Street.

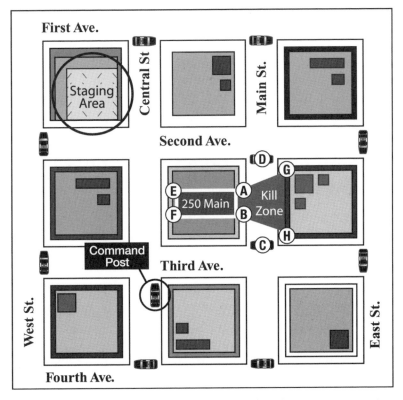

Figure 4-6: The staging area for additional resources must be in a controlled area and have good access to the scene.

The staging area is an absolute requirement. Create it and use it appropriately. Too often a supervisor phrases a request to dispatch as, "Send me a fire company and ambulance support." This directive results in the requested resource responding to the incident location. In other words, into the kill zone. The establishment of a staging area prevents this from occurring.

As when ordering in your initial resources, a sample transmission for the scenario depicted in Figure 4-6 might be: "I need fire and ambulance units standing by on Central Street between First and Second. They must avoid Main Street between Second and Third."

When you establish a staging area, don't forget to appoint a staging area supervisor. Resources directed to a staging area have a reasonable expectation to be met and briefed by a police representative. If you neglect to assign a staging area supervisor, you lose contact with and control over incoming resources. Responders will not stand by indefinitely without being briefed on the situation and tactics. Also, without the appointment of a staging area supervisor, the scene commander has a harder time finding out that requested resources have arrived and are available for deployment.

7. Identify and Request Additional Resources

Our final critical task is the identification of and call for additional resources. Although we treat it here at the end, keep in mind this doesn't necessarily mean it is the last task performed. You may determine the need for a SWAT or hazmat team response in the early moments of a critical incident. If so, make the call immediately.

Resources take time to mobilize and arrive at the scene. Therefore, the sooner you identify and request them, the sooner they will be ready for deployment. If the initial responding supervisor is not of a rank or position capable of authorizing the mobilization, then someone of that rank should be notified as soon as possible so they can authorize the requests. Resources available within the law enforcement discipline include specialty teams with training and expertise in specified areas of police response, such as:

- SWAT teams

- Hostage negotiators

- Bomb squads

Identify and request additional resources proactively. Do not simply request what you know you already need—brainstorm to predict what *might* be needed. The following sections include some examples and issues particular to non-police resources that you may activate for a critical incident.

Emergency Medical Services (EMS)

A crucial part of your job is anticipating and requesting EMS support, whether it is public or private, professional or volunteer. Waiting until someone is injured at a scene is too late. Surprisingly, time and again emergency police responders fail to proactively order these resources to stand by. This is especially true where the agency may be charged for the standby service. The result may be a bomb squad moving a suspicious device without a medical team on-scene. We think it's probably worth a few dollars to save the life of one or more of your bomb techs.

Critical incidents by their very nature pose a threat to the general public and to the emergency responders. Request EMS to stand by at the staging area for every critical incident regardless of initial need.

Fire Service

Although you are surely quick to recognize the need for fire response at a scene involving flames or hazardous material, you may overlook that need in what are generally considered "police scenes." Incidents involving barricaded gunmen, armed hostage scenes, and high-risk warrant executions are some examples of scenes where fire resources may not be routinely requested to stand by.

Again, think proactively. Most of the police scenes described above will be resolved with the deployment of a SWAT team. Specialized teams bring specialized equipment such as tear gas, "flash bang" diversionary devices, and/or explosive entry devices. Any or all of these gadgets are capable of starting fires, regardless of whatever nonflammable characteristics they may claim. If you know one or more of these tactics are being considered, have a fire company standing by in the staging area.

Additionally, fire companies bring tools and equipment law enforcement officers do not normally have available in their police vehicles. Ladders, supplemental lighting, SCBA, ropes, prybars, axes, and tarpaulins are just a few of the items that may prove exceedingly useful.

The Media

There is one resource that responds to the scene whether we request it or not—the media. Of course, most supervisors don't exactly see journalists as an asset. But think about it: today's media can establish instantaneous communication with our jurisdictions. They can provide the public with directions and instructions regarding your incident. Just a few examples include areas to avoid, recommended evacuation areas, and public refuge locations.

Don't think of reporters and cameramen as adversaries. That stale old prejudice simply forces them to find whatever story they can. They *will* get their story—with or without your input. Why not give them the story you want them to have, the actual story? Hopefully you have a well-equipped command post that will allow you to monitor what the media is reporting about your event. If you work with them correctly, the media can be invaluable for controlling rumors that can inflame your situation.

For purposes of the critical tasks, the main responsibility for the first responding supervisor is to direct all media representatives to the staging area. Note this is within your outer perimeter. It may seem self-evident, but keeping the media in a controlled area gives you at least some ability to manage them. Situating the media in the staging area has several excellent advantages.

- This gives your Information Officer (an ICS function that will be covered in Chapter Five; see page 109) a good location for conducting periodic news briefings.

- Reporters like to be where the decision-makers are. But you don't want them at your command post. The staging area provides a good backdrop for on-camera talent. They are safe yet they will not feel isolated from events.

- In general, the media has the same right of access as the general public. Granting the media staging area access gives them a privileged vantage point from which to broadcast. Use this privilege to ensure their cooperation. If a certain crew fails to comply with reasonable requests from commanders or fails to control their personnel, restrict that crew to beyond the outer perimeter. They would no longer have access to your briefings and would therefore be at a particular disadvantage in trying to cover your incident.

We walk a fine line between press access and scene security. Never allow live television broadcasting from the kill zone of any type of ongoing criminal activity. Such reports may endanger the lives of citizens and/or officers involved in the incident. For example, a "live eye" helicopter camera broadcasting deployment positions, arrival of additional resources, or other strategic information poses a definite and direct threat to both officers involved and citizens. One tragic example occurred during the coverage of a hostage incident in Berkeley, California. The suspect saw live broadcasts of SWAT teams deploying against his location and was prompted to shoot his hostages.

As a side note, most bomb squads prefer not to be photographed while addressing a suspected device. The equipment and strategies thus shown may aid a potential bomber to defeat their efforts the next time.

The "live eye" ban is a basic ground rule of critical incident management that your department should discuss with media representatives in your area before a critical incident occurs. The heat of an incident is not the time to try and establish ground rules for a good relationship. This is something you must work toward long before an incident arises.

Utility Companies

Power companies (gas and electric), telephone, television, water, and sewer are all examples of utility companies you may call on to resolve a critical incident. Let's examine a few situations in which their services might be required:

- **Power Companies.** Where a threat of fire or explosion exists, the need to terminate electric or gas service is readily apparent. Some supervisors believe terminating power to barricaded or armed hostage scenes is also standard operating procedure. This is not always the case. SWAT teams often prefer the power left on, especially at night. Power may also be bargaining chip for negotiators. Therefore, although you might call power authorities to the staging area, don't make the decision to terminate power to a scene without consulting the responding specialist.

- **Telephone Company.** Notify the local phone carrier, especially in hostage situations, as quickly as possible.

The ability to limit the incoming and outgoing calls to a specific phone is crucial. Unfortunately, to control cell phone calls we must have the specific number assigned to a phone.

- **Cable/Satellite Television.** The popularity of non-broadcast television gives us an additional option in critical incident management. Historically, one of the reasons given for cutting power to a location was to limit a suspect's ability to monitor television reports of the incident. Many late-model televisions are not capable of receiving a clear signal without benefit of a cable connection or external satellite dish. A single call to the service provider can result in termination. Providers frequently can do this right from the broadcast location and might not need to come on-scene.

These strategies are just a few of the many possibilities. Only the innovative thinking of the crisis manager limits the services utility companies can provide. Identify these resources as you begin to stabilize the crisis phase. Their response time will vary from location to location.

Official Resources vs. Realistic Resources

Most of the resources discussed to this point have been *official* resources. They are usually listed in resource manuals. The development of a quality resource manual is definitely worthwhile. But creating the manual is only the first step. Keeping it up to date and accurate is an ongoing responsibility. If your agency has such a document, do two things:

- Take it out and verify whether it has been updated recently. If not, call the numbers and check the names of the officials listed. You may be surprised to find how inaccurate your information is!

- Check on actual response times. Sure, a resource may be listed, but how much good is it going to do you if it can't get to your scene for eight hours? The availability (or non-availability) of a resource has a direct impact on your strategy planning.

Realistic resources are those that are available in your jurisdiction when you need them. These can be official or unofficial. Officers working in rural or isolated areas tend to be skilled at utilizing unofficial realistic resources. These officers learn to improvise simply because they don't have the resources available to urban officers. Conversely, urban officers frequently lack this skill because specialized backup is usually just a call away.

Put yourself in this position: You are responding to an in-progress crime scene where an officer has been wounded and extraction is imperative for survival. What could you use as a cover vehicle to rescue the victim?

If your agency does not address this question in the calm of pre-incident planning, someone in the emotion and confusion of a crisis will probably try to make the rescue without proper equipment or cover vehicle.

An official resource manual may list a State National Guard armored vehicle you could activate through official channels. This process will probably be time-consuming in the best of conditions. If your incident occurs on New Year's Eve it may be impossible. The armored vehicle becomes a non-resource for your incident.

On the other hand, your jurisdiction may contain a service garage for a private armored car company. If so, *before a crisis*, contact the manager and find out how you might be able to activate one of their armored cars in the event of an incident. (You'll also want to make sure it truly is armored!) Get home and/or pager numbers for the person with the keys. A little planning on your part may make available a *realistic* resource that can make the difference between life and death. The more we plan in advance, the less we will have to rely on reactive, spur-of-the-moment decisions when managing a critical incident.

Summary

It probably took us longer to explain these tasks than it would take you to actually implement them in the field. This is the crisis phase; things happen quickly. Your radio is blaring, your heart's pounding.

Remember, you have a universal game plan that calls for you to:

1. Establish control and communications

2. Identify the kill zone

3. Establish the inner perimeter

4. Establish the outer perimeter

5. Establish the on-scene command post

6. Establish a staging area

7. Identify and request additional resources

Take a deep breath and assume your tactical leadership persona. Focus on incident containment and perform your critical tasks.

Review Questions

1. If incidents share common characteristics, then you should be able to apply...what?

2. What are your primary goals in the crisis phase?

3. Can you think of how the Seven Critical Tasks would have applied to an incident in which you have participated?

4. What are the criteria for the appropriate placement of the command post and staging areas?

5. Can you think of some realistic resources you can call on in your jurisdiction?

Five

NIMS & ICS

Objectives

After completing this chapter, you should be able to:

- *Recall the major components of the National Incident Management System*

- *Describe the role and duties of the Incident Commander*

- *Recognize the functional areas of the Incident Command System*

- *Apply the Incident Command System to both planned events and unplanned critical incidents*

Events such as 9/11 have forced the United States to recognize that emergency response must be a coordinated effort at all levels of government. To address this need, the federal government developed the National Incident Management System (NIMS). All agencies—federal, state, and local—will be expected to comply with NIMS directives in any major response. The scene management strategies we discuss in this book are the *working end* of this national program.

A primary component of NIMS is the Incident Command System (ICS). You have probably heard of or attended training on ICS. However, it has not become as significant a component of law enforcement response as it has in the fire service. For whatever reason, law enforcement has not embraced ICS. Our goal for this chapter is show you what a powerful and flexible tool ICS can be for managing *your* critical incident. We want you to be comfortable with it for two reasons: 1) it is incredibly useful, and 2) regardless of the department or organization you represent, you are going to come under increasing pressure to show you've implemented ICS at least in certain responses (such as hazmat).

This chapter will quickly overview NIMS, give you a good feel for what ICS can do for you on just about any kind of scene, and then wrap up with how you can apply ICS to planned events in your community.

National Incident Management System

So what is NIMS? It's a directive straight from the White House. Here is an excerpt describing the system from *Homeland Security Presidential Directive/Hspd-5* issued February 28, 2003:

> *[The NIMS] will provide a consistent nationwide approach for Federal, State, and local governments to work effectively and efficiently together to prepare for, respond to, and recover from domestic incidents, regardless of cause, size, or complexity. To provide for interoperability and compatibility among Federal, State, and local capabilities, [The NIMS] will include a core set of concepts, principles, terminology, and technologies covering the incident command system; multi-agency coordination systems; unified command; training; identification and management of resources (including systems for classifying types of resources); qualifications and certification; and the collection, tracking, and reporting of incident information and incident resources.*

As you can see, NIMS operates at every level of response. Let's summarize the major components of NIMS:

- **Incident Command System.** An on-scene structure of management-level positions suitable for managing any type of critical incident.

- **Training.** Development and delivery of training courses for ICS and related topics.

- **Qualifications and Certification.** National standards for qualifications and certification for ICS positions.

- **Publications Management.** Development, control, sources, and distribution of NIMS publications.

- **Supporting Technology.** Technology and systems used to support an emergency response, such as remote automatic weather stations, infrared technology, and communications.

You may have heard of the National *Interagency* Incident Management System (NIIMS), which has been around since the 1980s. It may be a little confusing, but based on the presidential directive of 2003, NIMS replaces NIIMS.

Now we'll turn to the heart of NIMS, the Incident Command System.

Incident Command System (ICS)

ICS was initially developed by the Southern California fire service in the 1970s to coordinate wildfire management. Since then, the system has been expanded and enhanced to address critical incidents of any nature. Emergency agencies nationwide and at every level have adopted ICS.

Essentially, ICS allows you to quickly put together a "decision-making team" to manage major incidents. It is a highly flexible and modular organization structure built around the specific functions *you* need—from command to media liaison.

You can expand or contract the ICS structure according to the size, scope, and seriousness of the incident to be managed. You can also adapt it to accommodate the agencies involved and the objectives and strategies selected to control the incident. ICS can handle responses ranging from a single agency operating in its own jurisdiction to multiple agencies coordinating across multiple jurisdictions, from barricaded gunmen to hurricanes.

In this chapter we'll look at how you can actually use ICS in your responses, the structure and functions of ICS, and a variety of optional system elements you can bring to bear on your particular incidents. As mentioned before, a chapter in a book is no substitute for training. However, it will give you a good overview and some ideas about how you can realistically apply ICS.

ICS Operating Requirements

To help convince you ICS is relevant to your duties, let's take a look at the characteristics *required* of ICS. These are features of the command system identified as crucial to any response.

- **Adaptability.** ICS must be flexible enough to adapt to any emergency or incident. It has to be effective across the board.

- **Accessibility.** You as the responding supervisor have to be sold on the idea that ICS applies to your job. And the system has to be simple enough to be understood by all members of your organization.

- **Expandability.** ICS must be able to rapidly expand to serve your needs as an incident grows and changes. Similarly, ICS needs to be able to contract as specific job functions are no longer required.

- **Commonality.** Many critical incident responses will be joint efforts among federal and local public safety agencies. To avoid working at cross-purposes, each responding agency must use the same system. Therefore, the system must consist of common terminologies, organization, and procedures.

ICS was designed to be adaptable and easy to understand–and it is. But it's of no use to anyone if you don't practice it and use it on your scenes.

ICS Components

ICS is not complex, but it is complete. It consists of a number of components that may be familiar from your daily responses. You already know how valuable they are.

Confronting the whole system at once may seem a little overwhelming. But with some practice, you'll find each component serves a vital and logical function. The system works, or it wouldn't have lasted as long as it has.

The components include:

- Modular Organization

- Unified Command Structure

- Incident Action Plans

- Common Terminology

- Integrated Communications

- Manageable Span-of-Control

- Predesignated Incident Facilities

- Comprehensive Resource Management

We'll cover each one of these components in the context of the functional areas to which they best apply. For example, when we discuss the duties of the Incident Commander, we'll introduce you to Incident Action Plans and Unified Command structures.

As you go through this chapter, think back to incidents with which you've been involved and recall if you did or didn't use the ICS components. When would they have helped?

Modular Organization

Modularity is the core characteristic of ICS. ICS includes a common organization structure you can create in a "building block" fashion depending on the size and type of incident you face. Modular organization places initial responsibility with the Incident Commander (IC), then authorizes an Officer in Charge to lead each of the following sections:

- **Operations.** Responsible for all tactical operations of an incident. The Operations OIC directs the implementation of action plans and strategies for incident resolution.

- **Planning and Intelligence.** Responsible for collecting, evaluating, and disseminating information regarding an incident. The Planning OIC then works with the IC to plan an appropriate response. Planning staff asks the "what if" questions. What if this incident moves from daytime to nighttime—what resources will we need? While Operations manages the next ten to thirty minutes, Planning works in the next two to ten hours.

- **Logistics.** Responsible for providing all resources (personnel, equipment, facilities, services, etc.) required for incident management.

- **Finance.** Responsible for all cost and financial matters related to an incident. If you need to rent a crane or a bulldozer, you will need a Finance OIC.

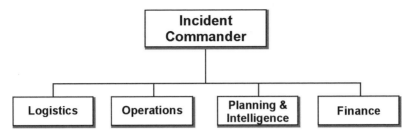

Figure 5-1: The basic Incident Command System structure.

As we have stressed, ICS provides a "toolbox" approach to managing critical events. You activate only the functions you need for a particular incident. Bear in mind ICS is about functions being performed, not people manning positions. If one individual (you!) can simultaneously manage all functional areas, then you don't need to bring other people on board.

Should you ever start to feel overwhelmed, however, get some help. As you add to the structure, one person may still manage more than one function. But should that person become overwhelmed, add additional command personnel to relieve the pressure.

What follows is a lot of org chart-type information, we know. You may never be involved in a fully expanded ICS structure. Let's hope not. But if and when it is required, you must be ready to implement or participate in an ICS response.

Incident Commander (IC)

Let's start at the top with the Incident Commander. The IC sets objectives and priorities. This person has the overall responsibility at the incident, including development of the Incident Action Plan, and the approval and release of all resources.

In many instances, the IC is the first responding supervisor. Of course, in the case of more serious incidents, a higher-ranking officer may relieve that person. If the original IC is relieved, he or she will likely be reassigned to another position, such as Operations OIC. It's nothing personal!

This book has spent a good many pages discussing the leadership characteristics essential for the crisis phase of a critical incident. Those techniques apply "pre-ICS." Once you move into the scene management phase, you will find the autocratic style is no longer effective.

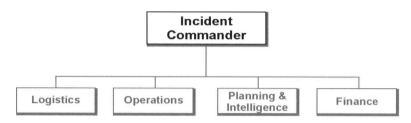

Figure 5-2: It all begins with the Incident Commander.

We'll abandon sports analogies for the moment. Now that you have a larger group to coordinate, we'll liken the IC to a symphony conductor. A conductor doesn't try to play every instrument. A conductor simply makes sure everyone is on the same page of the score (the Incident Action Plan), and ensures everyone starts, stays in tempo, and stops together.

If you do your job correctly, you should feel completely "underwhelmed." Everyone may seem busy but you. It will be an odd feeling. But this is the only way you can be sure to concentrate fully on the command function. If you are frantically developing a tactical plan to dislodge a barricaded gunman, how much attention do you have to spare for the other fifty incident developments that require your attention?

Your co-commanders and section officers must be competent or you wouldn't have appointed them. An IC is not a dictator or micromanager. An IC empowers subordinates. Let them do what they're paid to do. You wouldn't try to tell the bomb squad how to do their job, would you?

Incident Action Plan

We've already mentioned the Incident Action Plan (IAP) a couple of times. As the development of this plan is usually a large part of the IC's role, let's go into a little more detail. Usually, the IAP is the product of brainstorming among the Command, Operations, and Planning and Intelligence sections.

Don't get the idea that plan development is a major burden. For small incidents that you can wrap up quickly, you may not need to write down the plan. Just agree on it and go. However, there are cases when the plan *must* be in writing:

- **When multiple jurisdictions and/or agencies are involved.** Each jurisdiction and agency has a right to know how it will be impacted by the plan and how its resources will be used. A neighboring chief may need to know how his people are going to be utilized in your operations. You can just show him the plan!

- **When the incident requires shift changes.** You've probably solved problems and made decisions during your shift. Keep track of and update the plan, then hand it off to your relief personnel. Make sure the next shift doesn't reinvent the wheel.

It may seem unreasonable, but with the aid of the Planning and Intelligence section, the IC should always have a fallback plan if the situation changes suddenly. You can't plan for every contingency, but always ask a few of those "what if" questions.

Unified Command Structure

There is one more command-related concept we should cover while the IC function is still fresh in your mind. Incidents have no regard for jurisdictional boundaries. Hazmat spills and natural disasters, as well as many types of criminal activities, can quickly develop into multidiscipline and multi-jurisdictional events. Depending on the type of incident and its location, you may find yourself working with agencies such as fire and EMS as well as public safety agencies from other jurisdictions, at both the local and federal levels.

Unified command simply means that all agencies sharing responsibility for an incident contribute to that incident's resolution. To that end, all agencies have input into:

- Developing the overall Incident Action Plan and objectives

- Selecting strategies

- Planning tactical activities

- Performing integrated tactical operations

- Maximizing assigned resources

So who participates in a unified command? Well, it depends on the *location* of the incident (which determines the political or geographical jurisdictions involved) and the *kind* of incident (which determines the functional agencies involved). The command then usually consists of either a key responsible official from each jurisdiction or representatives from several functional departments within a single political jurisdiction.

Think of major events such as the Columbine High School tragedy, Hurricane Andrew, and the Oklahoma City bombing. In these cases, a unified command structure between local, state and (in some cases) federal agencies was required for effective incident resolution.

Be prepared to work with fire chiefs, EMS supervisors, and hazmat technicians as well as local politicians and other law enforcement agencies. Each brings unique skills and perspectives. Of course, each may bring a unique agenda, as well. As IC in a unified command, you may need to balance a wide range of opinions on objectives and tactics.

Now that you have some familiarity with ICS command structures, we will turn to the four functional areas the IC can establish to control and resolve a situation. It is critical that you understand these functions so you'll know what you should expect from your team.

Within each functional area there are several staff positions you may need filled. To help clarify expectations, Appendix A provides a checklist of each position's tasks (see page 153). If necessary, give subordinates the checklists so *they* know what you expect of them.

At a minimum, make sure the people you work with know their responsibilities and stick to them. It will take discipline. Remember, you are building a team and each role is important for the successful management of the event.

Operations Section

Operations is the section where police officers tend to be most comfortable. It's where most of us have worked for the bulk of our careers. Whenever you find yourself setting up an ICS response, expect supervisors to gravitate to this area.

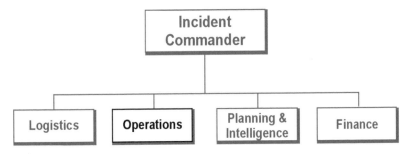

Figure 5-3: Operations rolls up its sleeves and directly controls the incident.

This section runs the units that are directly responsible for tactical incident stabilization and resolution. Operations and the Operations OIC are charged with short-term, tactical thinking and related input on the IAP.

The nature of the incident determines the makeup of the Operations section. If your incident is a criminal activity, Operations will be composed of law enforcement personnel. If it is a fire or hazmat scene, this section will be made up of fire or hazmat personnel.

Reporting to the Operations OIC are the Mission Unit Leaders. These individuals lead the front-line response specialists (SWAT, Canine Unit, Mounted Unit, Hazardous Materials Response Unit, etc.). They coordinate with other mission unit leaders to implement the IAP.

Manageable Span-Of-Control

That leads us to another hallmark of ICS: management span of control. In general, ICS span-of-control guidelines say that any individual with emergency management responsibility should be able to effectively manage from three to seven subordinates. That averages out to five. Obviously, there are exceptions to this rule. Effective span-of-control can be influenced by several factors:

- Type of incident

- Nature of the task

- Hazards and safety factors

- Distances between elements

One important span-of-control consideration is to anticipate change and prepare for it. This is especially true during the rapid buildup of resources at the beginning of an event. Planning is critical at this point to avoid runaway ordering of resources and overloading your mission unit leaders. Remember, a key feature of ICS is the ability to expand your response forces rapidly and maintain appropriate span of control.

One resource that should be used regularly is the Operations Dispatcher. The Operations Dispatcher reports to the Operations OIC and serves as communications coordinator for all radio traffic at the command post.

The Operations Dispatcher is crucial for making sure all commands by the Operations OIC are verbalized at the command post. The Operations OIC does not deliver orders over the radio personally, but directs the dispatcher to relay them. This allows others, such as the Safety Officer (SO), to monitor operational orders and provide input before orders get to the field.

An example of an Operations OIC delivering orders directly on the radio might be:

> *Operations OIC into radio*: "Car 20, perform task A-B-C."
> *SO to Operations OIC*: "Hold it, you can't do that."
> *Operations OIC into radio*: "Car 20 standby."
> *Operations OIC to SO*: "Why not?…Oh, I see."
> *Operations OIC into radio*: "Car 20, disregard previous order. Perform task D-E-F."

If the Operations OIC verbalizes the order before going to the radio, the Safety Officer has a chance to intervene, if necessary. Funnel all commands and directives from the command post through the Operations Dispatcher.

Planning and Intelligence Section

Planning and Intelligence does what you'd expect. These individuals, led by the Planning OIC, are responsible for finding out everything the IC could possibly need to know about an incident. This might include identifying high-risk locations, identifying persons inciting violence, estimating damage/injury/casualty situations, and monitoring weather and environmental conditions.

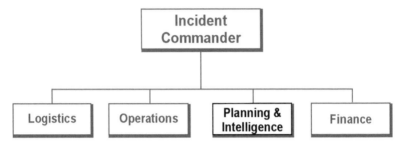

Figure 5-4: Planning and Intelligence anticipates the little surprises that can trip up a response.

Planning and Intelligence also asks "what if" questions. For example, during the tragedy at Columbine High School in 1999, the Planning OIC might have asked, "What if this school *isn't* the primary target?" What if the school attack had been a diversionary tactic and the actual target had been a raid on the US Mint or the Federal courthouse? It can be very useful to have someone thinking that way when all other resources are tightly focused on a specific event.

"What if" questions needn't be that seemingly far out. They could be as mundane as asking, "What if this incident lasts into the night?" When a unit calls in to the command post at dusk and requests lights, you don't want to have to tell them it will take two hours. You want to be able to say the lights are standing by in the staging area. Your teams will appreciate it! Planning and Intelligence should develop a wish list of resources and work closely with Logistics, which we'll discuss next.

The Planning and Intelligence function uses the information it gathers to help the IC develop the Incident Action Plan and at least one backup plan. It also prepares a plan for both responders and the public to return to normal operations.

Logistics Section

The Logistics section makes sure you have what you need when you need it. It is a proactive function. Logistics should work with other sections to determine early on what facilities, services, and resources might be required to support incident resolution.

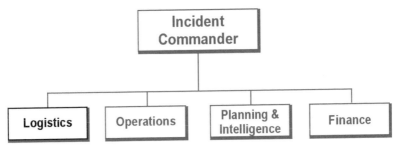

Figure 5-5: Logistics holds the whole show together with infrastructure and services.

One of the key Logistics responsibilities is maintaining the staging area. You may recall that establishing a staging area is one of your Seven Critical Tasks. The Logistics OIC appoints a Staging Area Supervisor to manage the location to which personnel and equipment are sent before being put into service. This supervisor briefs incoming resources and maintains a status log of all available and deployed resources.

Comprehensive Resource Management

That leads us to another ICS component: comprehensive resource management. You may have hundreds of responders in dozens of vehicles at your scene. You don't want to lose track of them. According to a briefing we received from the Operations OIC at the Oklahoma City bombing in 1993, forty firefighters were staged and then overlooked for two hours. You can avoid this sort of thing by maintaining strict accountability, such as through a Logistics assignment board that tracks the status and current condition of all resources. Note where the resource is and how long it's been there. Don't leave a unit in position for twelve hours without relief!

Logistics should update the other sections on resource changes that affect their areas of accountability. For example, if no backup units are available for a certain operational tactic, the Operations OIC had better know about it.

Pre-Designated Incident Facilities

Another key ICS concept is utilizing predesignated incident facilities. You don't have to make Logistics come up with your entire support structure on the fly. For example, when you need to manage a critical event, you don't want to also have to create a functional command post from the ground up. (If you have a mobile command post, use it!) And command posts are just *one* of the facility types you may need on a major critical incident. You may need staging areas, mass care centers, and evacuation centers, just to name a few.

Each incident dictates the required facilities and the appropriate locations. Once you institutionalize ICS, you and your Logistics OIC will be able to plan ahead and identify facilities that will be available to you as soon as an incident occurs.

Integrated Communications

Yet another fundamental ICS concept related to Logistics is the need for integrated communications. Logistics is responsible for much of the communications that takes place at a scene.

Simply put, every agency, section, and unit should be able to talk to every other agency, section, and unit. And for that you need a plan and a communications center established solely for the resources assigned to the incident.

The Communications Unit, under the Communications Supervisor (who reports to the Logistics OIC), is responsible for all communications planning for the incident. This includes scene-specific radio networks, on-site telephones, public address systems, and off-site incident telephone/microwave/radio systems.

In a perfect world, we recommend radio networks for large incidents be organized as follows:

- **Command Frequency.** This frequency links the Incident Command, key command staff members, section officers, and key supervisors.

- **Tactical Frequency.** There may be several tactical frequencies. The Logistics section may assign them based on agencies, departments, geographical areas, or even specific functions.

- **Support Frequency.** Use this frequency to direct resources and support any other non-tactical or command functions.

In any case, responders should confine communications to essential messages only. And as was mentioned earlier, all communications should be in plain text, not ten codes.

Logistics is responsible for a couple of additional areas as well. The Logistics OIC oversees:

- **Security Unit Supervisor.** Coordinates the activities of the security unit and supervises assigned personnel. You'll need someone to secure the command post, staging area, and other areas.

- **Personnel Group Supervisor.** Evaluates personnel requirements, maintains a master listing of personnel assignments, and performs time-keeping functions.

As one general is credited with saying, "Operations is for amateurs, *logistics* is for the pros." Even the best plan cannot be successfully executed if it's not supported logistically.

Finance Section

Somebody has to pay for all of this! A large-scale incident can present dozens of financial considerations you don't want to have to think about. You want to focus on your scene. The Finance section provides emergency purchase orders to pay for any resources ordered.

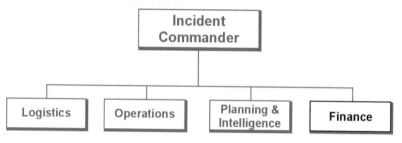

Figure 5-6: Finance foots the bills (or at least sees to it that everyone gets paid!)

The Finance OIC reports to the IC and performs all financial and cost analysis of the incident. Finance also performs record-keeping and administrative duties. Subordinate finance functions may include the Time Unit, Procurement Unit, Compensation Claims Unit, and Cost Unit.

Staff Positions

In addition to the four functional sections, ICS provides for a number of additional staff positions to support a response. These staff positions are:

- Deputy Incident Commander

- Safety Officer

- Incident Log/Scribe

- Information Officer

- Liaison Officer and Agency Representatives

As before, the IC activates only those positions that are needed. One person can hold down multiple positions as long as that person is not overwhelmed.

Deputy Incident Commander

The Deputy Incident Commander is the second in command. In smaller incidents this function certainly may not be required. In larger incidents, though, a Deputy IC is a must. If the IC needs to leave the scene to meet with the mayor, the deputy assumes control. Therefore, a deputy needs to be aware of all the leadership issues associated with the IC position.

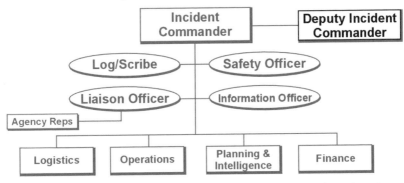

Figure 5-7: The Deputy IC manages the command post and steps in whenever the IC is unavailable.

The deputy acts a "systems manager" for the command post, making sure things run smoothly. Activities include coordinating section heads, reviewing status reports, and making sure all unit logs get submitted to the IC on a time.

Safety Officer

The Safety Officer role is integral to fire response, but it has to be one of the most frequently overlooked positions in law enforcement. The Safety Officer is *not* interested in the safety of the general public. The SO focuses exclusively on responders. He or she assesses the Incident Action Plan and proposed tactics with *nothing* in mind but the safety of responders. This is the person who checks the wind before a tear gas assault and makes sure all officers have proper cover.

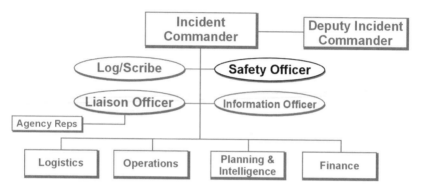

Figure 5-8: The Safety Officer can yell "Stop!" if responders are in unnecessary danger.

When this officer finds an unsafe condition or planned action on the scene, it is his or her duty to bring the problem to the IC's attention. If time or other developments do not permit that, the SO has the authority under ICS to unilaterally stop all activity. We mean *everything*. If the SO says *No*, that particular task does not go forward.

As you can imagine, you don't want a shrinking violet or "yes man" in this position. You need an officer with an assertive but nonabrasive personality. We frequently use a good SO as an example of a round peg for that round hole. It's wonderful when there's a fit. (On larger incidents, the SO function can be filled jointly by representatives from law, fire, EMS, etc. Each will have primary responsibility for his or her own department personnel.)

It is our opinion that you should *never* run a critical incident scene without an SO. And when you create the position, don't make that person multitask. Let the SO focus exclusively on what he or she is there for: to save lives. This is so important we will say it again:

> *The Safety Officer is not interested in the safety of the general public. The SO focuses exclusively on the safety of responders.*

An example of not taking this function into account is the Bureau of Alcohol, Tobacco and Firearms (ATF) 1993 raid on the Branch Davidian Compound at Waco, Texas. (The source for this analysis is the Treasury Department report of September 1993.) The two requirements for the raid to go forward were:

1. The ATF must have had the element of surprise, and

2. Upon ATF arrival, the men of the compound must have been outside of the buildings.

As we all found out afterwards, the raid occurred despite the fact that *both* of these requirements were not met.

The ATF raid plan, from what we could determine, did not include a Safety Officer. Therefore, no one had the authority under ICS to say, "Stop! They know we're coming!" Tragically, gunfire from the compound killed four ATF agents.

Incident Log/Scribe

The Incident Log/Scribe is a command staff function that maintains a record of the event and the decisions taken to resolve it. As you can imagine, the Scribe must be a good listener. This is not a court reporter type of function. Although the Scribe may not be a law enforcement officer, it helps if the person has a good understanding of critical incident procedures. This helps the Scribe focus on important developments instead of getting bogged down in irrelevant detail.

In the past, this person had to have good handwriting skills. These days, the Scribe will probably have a laptop computer and the ability to project the log on the wall.

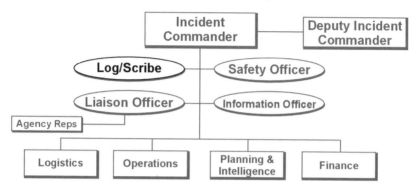

Figure 5-9: The Scribe ensures there is an accurate record of all events and decisions.

The question of keeping audio or video logs comes up frequently in our training sessions. While both may be used, neither precludes the need for a written event log. Although videotapes can be "time burned," as IC it would be difficult to quickly check a tape (audio or video) for the exact time a directive was given or a request made. The written log can be checked easily at the scene.

Frequently, you'll see the IC turn to the Scribe at a critical point in the event to make sure they've made note of the issue, the decision, and the time. As we've mentioned before, the log can be critical for the post-incident debriefing and any civil or criminal reviews that take place.

The Scribe is also responsible for creating and maintaining a map of the incident area. If possible, the Scribe should project this map from an overhead transparency or computer program so the entire staff can see it.

You can think of the incident log as the master record of command decisions. But keep in mind that *every one* of the command positions and functional areas is responsible for its own log. As you've read about each of these functional areas, did you think about the myriad individual decisions, problems, and triumphs they could encounter over the course of a critical incident? All must be recorded for accountability and analysis.

Information Officer

The Information Officer is responsible for formulating and releasing (with IC approval) all information regarding the incident to the media and other personnel.

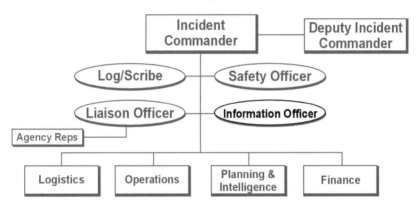

Figure 5-10: The Information Officer keeps the media informed and off the IC's back.

The IO is your primary media point of contact. This person provides press releases and news conferences as necessary. If appropriate, the IO coordinates interviews between the media and other responders on scene. You want this type of access as tightly controlled as possible.

We've mentioned that an individual can handle multiple ICS functions, but there is one important exception: *the IC should not be the Information Officer.* In the first place, you don't want to take time away from managing the situation to talk to the press. Secondly, the IO can always plead ignorance when faced with tough questions. That is not an option for a commander. The IC should only address the press when the incident is concluded.

The IO doesn't necessarily have to be a member of the police department. It helps, but it's not a requirement.

Liaison Officer and Agency Representatives

The Liaison Officer helps initiate mutual aid agreements and serves as the point of contact between the IC and assisting agencies. This is the person on your staff who knows everyone and has the best "people" skills.

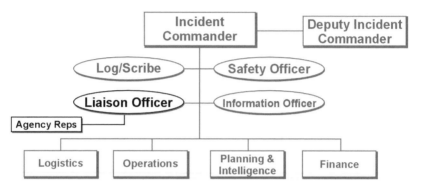

Figure 5-11: The Liaison Officer helps ensure all agencies and jurisdictions seamlessly work together.

The Liaison Officer works closely with representatives from each responding agency. These agency representatives are (or should be) empowered to provide the IC with whatever resources may be required. If you need a fire company, the fire service rep can activate the engines from staging and can relay orders. If you need ambulances, the EMS rep will get them. In fact, agency reps should be able to make any and all decisions regarding their departmental resources. Reps who must go back to their individual agency leaders to verify decisions create an unacceptable waste of time.

Reps can make invaluable contributions, from the formulation of the Incident Action Plan to the efficient demobilization of resources. However, there should be only one rep from each involved agency at the command post. This keeps down the head count at the command post and eliminates confusion as to whom the IC should go to for support requests.

The agency representatives report to the Liaison Officer or directly to the IC if the Liaison is not available.

Common Terminology

The fact we require a Liaison Officer and agency reps indicates the need for another ICS cornerstone concept: common terminology. Common terminology is one of those obvious requirements for a system used by multiple agencies. It's unlikely the FBI and a county sheriff's office are going to use the same terms to describe every element at a critical incident. But if you use ICS terms when talking with representatives from another agency, you're sure to be understood.

Organizational Summary

That wraps it up for the ICS organization. Below is a chart of a fully expanded ICS structure, which hopefully you will never have to implement. But if you do, you know that each function has specific duties and there is little or no overlap of responsibility. And don't forget that Appendix A has checklists of specific duties for each function (see page 153).

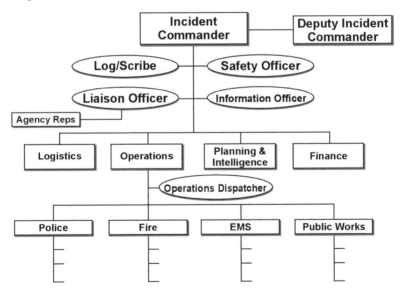

Figure 5-12: A fully expanded ICS structure. Usually, only large-scale incidents lead to the activation of every function.

Using ICS for Planned Events

Beyond giving you a powerful tool for managing the unexpected, ICS can aid you in preparing for and executing planned events. As we've mentioned before, we constantly review and evaluate critical incidents that have occurred across the United States and abroad. Again and again we find police agencies in most cases do *not* follow ICS guidelines when planning for major events in their communities. Many of those planned events turned into critical incidents, catching responsible agencies totally and completely unprepared.

ICS makes your life so much easier! But you have to implement it. Here are some examples of the types of events for which ICS can provide your agency with a planning and operations framework:

- Major drug raids or high-risk warrant service operations

- Annual community events that attract large crowds

- Demonstrations or planned civil disobediences at which you expect large crowds

- Major concerts or sporting events

Why reinvent the wheel or run the risk of missed assignments each time you have one of these occasions?

As you now know, ICS gives you a blueprint for placing agency personnel in key planning and management functions. You also have a command and response structure in place that you can expand rapidly to deal with whatever happens. We will discuss several essential functions you must activate when planning a major event, such as Incident Commander, Safety Officer, Operations OIC, etc. The size of the planning team will depend on the type of event for which you are organizing.

This team planning method also helps prevent your organization from being dependent upon one officer knowing how to handle, say, the traffic patterns you might expect at a festival. If only one person understands a certain "detail," that knowledge can leave your organization with that person. Get this critical knowledge in writing!

We'll use the example of a major, multi-act rock festival to highlight functions you should activate and the tasks and potential developments you must address.

- **Incident Commander.** As in a spontaneous incident, the IC assembles a team to ensure the Incident Action Plan is not only operationally sound, but also considers all alternatives, is supported logistically, and is as safe as possible for those charged with implementing the plan. The IC makes sure all functions are filled and that everyone is comfortable with their duties.

- **Incident Log/Scribe.** This person can track responsibility for activities during the planning process. Additionally, this person drafts any orders or directives regarding the event and collects all information gathered during the planning process. The Scribe should make sure that responders working the scene of our rock festival have access to the primary plan and all contingency plans.

- **Safety Officer.** The SO lays down basic requirements or prohibits certain activities that affect responder safety. These safety characteristics certainly apply to our rock festival. The SO might look at issues such as EMS support and how officers could be backed up for crowd control, if necessary.

- **Information Officer.** The IO manages vital information that must be released to the public before an event. For example, we would probably work with concert organizers to restrict what people can and cannot bring into the concert for security reasons. If large backpacks or glass bottles will be prohibited, the IO should get this information to the media well beforehand. Restricted parking, access routes, or public gathering areas will be easier to manage if those attending the festival have the information before the event. Having one point of contact also ensures security for confidential information you may not want made public.

- **Operations Officer.** This individual is responsible for making the plan happen on the street. Historically in non-ICS managed responses, this person was forced to perform all of the functions we have described, from media contact to logistics. By utilizing ICS, you can allow this individual to concentrate on plan execution, such as crowd and traffic control.

- **Planning and Intelligence Officer.** Bottom line…you don't want any surprises. To help avoid the unexpected, Planning and Intelligence might examine past music festival events. If you find out that a certain act attracts rowdier fans, you can plan for it. You will be prepared to respond or perhaps restrict activities to prevent a reoccurrence of a critical incident that occurred during a previous festival. The possibility that you will have to deal with an unexpected situation can never be totally eliminated, but it is greatly reduced when you staff this function.

- **Logistics.** Staffing this function ensures you will have all of the people, equipment, and other assets needed to successfully implement your plan. Preplanning logistics eliminates the need to scramble for resources in a hurried or panic mode. Also, non-emergency purchasing is usually more cost-effective. Just a few requirements of our festival might include barricades, overtime personnel, portable lights, and commissary facilities.

Implementing ICS for planned events allows you to develop a *comprehensive* plan rather than simply focusing on reactive tactics or operations. The various command staff and sections work independently to develop their own plan segments. These independent segments combine to produce one final all-inclusive plan for the event that no one commander or section head could come up with on his or her own.

As you begin to use ICS to prepare for major events in your community, you will quickly find it is the only way to develop a comprehensive and defensible response.

Summary

That's it for our quick tour of the personnel, structure, and application of the Incident Command System. These are functions our experience has shown us to be critical to law enforcement responses. You may not need all of it for each incident, but you should at least know what ICS can bring to bear on your incidents.

The bottom line for you as the IC is to understand how ICS can help *you* and to plan, plan, plan. Then act swiftly and sensibly. Your response should follow the old carpenter's maxim: Measure twice and cut once.

Review Questions

1. Can you recall the major components of the National Incident Management System?

2. Can you describe the management style of an ICS Incident Commander?

3. Can you describe the four primary functional ICS areas and at least three staff positions?

4. Can you recall the benefits of using ICS to prepare for planned events?

Six

Hazardous Materials and Weapons of Mass Destruction

Objectives

After completing this chapter, you should be able to:

- *Identify unique threats presented by various hazardous materials*

- *Describe the differences between accidental and intentional releases*

- *Apply the Seven Critical Tasks to a hazmat scene*

- *List response strategies specific to hazmat threats*

It may seem unusual, but we'll start this chapter by telling you what we're *not* going to do. The goal here is *not* to replicate traditional hazmat training. No single chapter can do that. While the following pages will touch on much of the same material you might expect at an awareness-level class, the presentation restricts itself to information required by an initial responding law enforcement supervisor, one who is forced to make critical decisions in the early stages of an event.

We've filtered this information over the years. Distilled it, if you will, into those factors that most directly affect your area of interest.

As we are all too aware, hazmat incidents can be accidental or intentional. In either case your response in the crisis phase will be exactly the same. Therefore, by improving your response to *all* critical incidents, you automatically improve your response to terrorist attacks. Although this chapter will focus on accidental releases, keep in mind the crisis phase strategies discussed apply to weapons of mass destruction (WMD) attacks as well.

The primary differences between accidental and intentional releases are in the details. With an intentional release, you may have criminal activity to control while you worry about the hazmat aspects. You may have criminal investigations to conduct afterwards. Regardless, in the crisis phase you always use the same basic game plan.

Our hope is that this chapter will have something for everybody. Even if you already have advanced hazmat certifications, you may still find our emphasis on practical, layman's response strategies useful.

The Method to Our Madness

A police officer is the first responder on-scene in the overwhelming majority of hazmat incidents. Yet, hazmat response training traditionally gets second-class treatment in many departments. Law enforcement tends to think of it as a fire responsibility. It certainly can be, but what you as the first-responding police supervisor need to realize is that the decisions *you* make during the crisis phase of a hazmat incident can determine the course of the event and the eventual toll it takes.

This chapter will focus on absolutely must-know information. You've probably been through at least hazmat awareness level training. You've probably sat in front of an authority from the fire service and been presented with hours of perfectly true and excellent information. Your eyes probably glazed over at some point. Listening to a hazmat expert can be a lot like listening to a neurosurgeon. It can be overwhelming.

We are not hazmat technicians. Our expertise and experience lie in the initial response as law enforcement supervisors. We focus on what you need to do in the first moments of any critical incident, be it criminal or chemical.

Our goal is to change your perceptions of hazmat incidents, to make you paranoid. Our goal is to help you protect yourself, the people that work for you, and the citizens you have sworn to serve.

Fire and Law

Before we get into the nuts and bolts of our discussion, we would like to address one of our pet issues: fire/law coordination. Our classes frequently include both fire and law responders with ranks ranging from sergeant to chief. We always conduct the same exercise. We ask the police (sitting on their side of the room): "How many of you train with fire?" Maybe one chief that attended a joint ICS class raises a hand. We then ask the same question of the fire service representatives. Same response.

Then we ask: "How many of you respond with the other department on critical incidents?" Every hand goes up.

Fire and law enforcement must work together on *all* critical incidents, but hazmat in particular dictates a multidisciplinary response. There must be improved communications and tactical coordination between these two most vital community services. As the world becomes a more dangerous place, anything less than a perfect working relationship is unacceptable.

We strongly recommend joint training programs. Don't wait to be told to do it. Be proactive.

Classes of Hazardous Materials

Here we go. A hazardous material is defined as any product, chemical, or substance that can cause damage or injury to life, the environment, or property when inappropriately released from its container. Our society runs on hazardous materials. They are in our stores, rolling down our streets, and in our homes.

We'll start this discussion with a quick overview of the kinds of materials you are likely to encounter. These materials are divided into nine classes that you probably had to memorize for your awareness certification. For our purposes, it is not critical that you be able to recall them in order. What you *should* be able to do is recognize the particular threat that each represents.

Unfortunately, just about any of these materials has the potential to become a WMD in the wrong hands. An explosion at a water treatment plant might result in a chlorine cloud smothering an entire neighborhood. This could be just as terrifying as an anthrax release at a busy airport terminal. Many of our most common hazardous materials are readily accessible and represent the basis for low-tech weapons.

Essentially, the primary threats from these materials fall into three types: fire, explosion, and health. It's enormously important you understand the nature of the threat so you can take appropriate action.

Most of the classes are further divided into divisions. We've thrown in sample materials for each class and division. As we'll discuss later, each of the classes is represented by one or more unique placards with dedicated colors and numbers. These are the intimidating skull-and-crossbones signs you see on the trucks that pass you doing 90 m.p.h. on the highway.

- **Class 1: Explosives.** There are six divisions that range from a mass explosion hazard (1.1-black powder) to low (1.6-fertilizer).

- **Class 2: Gases.** Three divisions include flammable (2.1-propane), nonflammable (2.2-anhydrous ammonia), and poisonous (2.3-phosgene). Flammable or nonflammable? This information is critical for state troopers in the habit of dropping flares at accident scenes.

- **Class 3: Flammable Liquids.** Examples include gasoline, kerosene, and diesel fuel. These are some of the most commonly transported hazardous materials.

- **Class 4: Flammable Solids, Spontaneously Combustible Materials, and Materials Dangerous When Wet.** These are solids that burn (4.1-magnesium); ignite when brought into contact with air (4.2-phosphorous), or that react badly to water (4.3-calcium carbonate). That last division is an odd one; some materials actually combust or give off toxic gases when wet. Think the fire department would like that information before they start spraying?

- **Class 5: Oxidizers and Organic Peroxides.** Some materials create their own oxygen and therefore burn more actively (5.1-ammonium nitrate) or contain oxygen in a certain chemical combination (5.2-ethyl ketone peroxide). What is ethyl ketone peroxide, you ask?…a good reason to have an *Emergency Response Guidebook* in your unit! (See Appendix B on page 175.)

- **Class 6: Poisons and Etiologic Materials.** The chemical industry uses a number of poisons to make up common compounds (6.1-arsenic). These substances are more prevalent than most of us care to know. *Etiologic* refers to infectious agents (6.2-hepatitis). Perhaps more than any other class, this last is most closely associated with terrorism. If you're dealing with a biological attack, you can guess it won't be placarded! Look for clues in bystanders, such as difficulty breathing. You will need to rely on your wits and training to assess the situation from a distance to avoid succumbing yourself.

- **Class 7: Radioactive Materials.** Transport hazards range from small amounts of medical radioactive materials to depleted uranium reactor rods. Any of these could be used to produce radiological weapons or so-called "dirty bombs." We're guessing you don't keep a Geiger counter in the trunk of your squad car. If you even suspect a radiological hazard, back off and call for help.

- **Class 8: Corrosives.** A corrosive is defined as any liquid or solid that eats away at human skin or a liquid that severely corrodes steel or aluminum. Sulfuric acid is a commonly transported corrosive.

- **Class 9: Miscellaneous Hazardous Materials.** A label with this on it isn't terribly informative. At least you'll know what a load *isn't* (flammable liquid, explosive, etc.). The definition of class 9 is fairly technical and includes substances like PCBs and asbestos.

Identifying Hazardous Materials

The placards for these classes are just one means of identifying materials. They cannot always be relied upon, however. For one thing, you won't find them on buildings that you may *know* contain hazardous materials. For another, transports may be improperly placarded. (This is a serious offense and many states have units dedicated to enforcing placarding laws.) Some placards are of the "flip" type and an accident may cause them to flip to another ID number, leading to misidentification and inappropriate action.

First, how do you *not* identify materials? There is some well-known footage of a major city battalion chief walking right up to a railway tanker leaking an unknown substance. After swiping his finger through the ooze and sniffing it, he *tastes* it! That just about covers every technique of how *not* to identify hazardous materials.

In law enforcement, we frequently hear the terms "cop-o-meter" and "blue canary." This is the officer that rushes into a scene or stands in a cloud directing traffic with eyes streaming and throat burning. Up clumps a hazmat technician in full Level A containment and asks the officer to describe his or her symptoms. Don't let this happen!

These illustrations aren't meant to be derogatory, but they do show a failure to realize that in most cases we are not dispatched to a hazmat scene, but rather to an MVA or industrial accident. It is usually only after the "blue canary" discovers the hazard that fire and hazmat specialists are notified. Without proper notification, *they* may well drive unprotected into a scene. Regardless, law enforcement must learn to react quicker and smarter once we have any indication of a hazmat situation. Traditionally we stay too close for too long. Our initial response should be best described using the EMS expression "load and go": Exit the scene as soon as possible and take anyone you can safely grab with you.

There are six acceptable methods for recognizing hazardous materials. Note that hazmat teams require at least three of these before initiating an action based on the material type.

- **Department of Transportation (DOT) Placards or Labels.** These placards are required by law and must meet certain size, shape, color, and position requirements. They are your first and best option for identifying transported materials.

- **Markings, Symbols, or Colors.** Beyond placarding, also look for common symbols and colors, such as orange for explosives, red for flammable, and skull and crossbones for poisons. Beware of military vehicles, which will probably have no markings of any kind. If you see a military transport on its side and the driver hotfooting away at top speed, that's a bad thing.

- **Bills of Lading or Shipping Papers.** All modes of transport must carry papers detailing the nature of on-board hazardous materials. (For whatever reason, these papers have a different title depending on whether you find them on a ship, truck, plane, or train.) Bills of lading, for example, should be kept in the cabs of all trucks carrying hazardous materials. Of course, you can't run up and grab them if the tank contents are pouring out!

- **Occupancy or Destination.** You can make some educated guesses about the contents of a building based on the nature of the business. Similarly, you can guess that a tank truck heading into a refinery might be carrying crude oil or petroleum additives.

- **Type or Shape of Container or Carrier.** Is the trailer you see on the highway designed for solids, liquids, or gases? Are the containers strewn across the interstate cardboard boxes, 55-gallon drums, or steel-reinforced concrete casks?

- **Environmental Detection Equipment.** This is the surest way to determine exactly what you might be facing. Of course, equipment sophisticated enough to determine material natures and concentrations are usually only found with hazmat specialists. If you're lucky enough to have some of this equipment in the trunk of your car, get in the habit of using it!

The caution exhibited by a hazmat team is similar to the intelligence gathering conducted by a SWAT team prior to taking action. In both cases the "specialists" will not act unless they have sufficient information to maximize their chances for success. They make informed decisions.

Where We Find Hazardous Materials

Simply put, hazmat threats are just about everywhere. You find them in both fixed locations and moving down our roadways, waterways, and airways. Commercially and privately. Each location presents its own particular risks and challenges to the first responder.

The number of chemicals and materials used in daily life has increased manyfold during the last generation. Common objects that used to be made of natural materials, such as your sofa cushions and your kids' toys, are now made from synthetics. These materials have complex components that start at plants, change chemical and physical form, get transported, and end up in your homes.

Our society runs on hazardous materials. Let's look at some of the common places you might encounter hazmat incidents and some first-responder considerations.

Commercial Locations

Do you know what goes on in your jurisdiction? Do you have chemical plants and industrial parks in your area? Frequently, you're not even allowed on commercial industrial property. Processes and components are often proprietary. Nevertheless, you had better educate yourself quickly if you're faced with a fire or other incident at any kind of production facility. Locate a plant manager or safety manager and get a list of the materials that may be involved.

One particularly handy piece of paper is the Material Safety Data Sheet (MSDS). Each chemical that rolls out of a production facility has such a sheet listing the material's full name, reactivity, hazards, and other useful information. If you're lucky, the plant manager will be able to tell you the primary hazards and then produce a book of these sheets. You can then hand it off to the specialist.

But dangerous substances are not limited to plants and industrial parks. As you know if you've ever gone shopping, many stores (particularly large discount stores) can have a huge range of potentially hazardous materials. They carry everything from nail polish to brake fluid. Just a few other places with specialty materials include photography shops, hobby shops, garden shops, dry cleaners, and agricultural supply stores.

Colleges, particularly research universities, also represent a wide range of possible threats. A few campuses have nuclear reactors, many have biological research programs, and most have chemical facilities. And what kind of security do you think most of these campuses have? Would it compare to military or even industrial security? Probably not.

Transportation Vehicles

Airplanes, trucks, railroad cars, and ships. Each jurisdiction has its own transport hazards. If you're lucky, the load laying in the middle of the highway will be placarded and the placard will be visible. You can then make the correct decisions to control the incident and preserve life.

Question: What is perhaps the most dangerous vehicle to find involved in a bad accident? *Answer*: A parcel delivery semitrailer or aircraft. These vehicles carry mixed loads of small quantities of substances ranging from radiological to infectious. And because the shipped quantities are frequently *just* below federal minimums, no placarding is required!

There is an unfortunate effect known in chemistry as "synergy." Normally we think of synergy as a good thing, but in this case the term refers to the fact there is no way to predict the behavior or characteristics of randomly mixed chemicals.

The danger of synergy applies not only to parcel transport, but also to delivery trucks associated with large discount stores. These semis could contain paints, thinners, ammunition, bulk photo-developing chemicals, pool chemicals, beauty aides, and automotive fluids just to name a few. Mix them all together and what have you got? Now, just to add some additional realism, imagine them on fire. You probably don't want your people walking through *that* cloud.

Illegal Drug Labs

Drug labs fall into both fixed and mobile categories. They can show up anywhere, from a rundown motel by the railroad tracks to a million-dollar home in a ritzy neighborhood to a fancy camper rolling down your interstate. Methamphetamine production in particular is widespread and generates enormous profits. Although produced from over-the-counter ingredients, when combined and cooked, these processes yield a laundry list of highly toxic substances.

You cannot run into a suspected drug lab without SCBA and some sort of protection suit. You've heard about the booby traps, but more likely than not it's the atmosphere that will put you in the hospital. Get trained and be careful.

Miscellaneous

How many other locations can you think of for hazardous materials? How about public and private swimming pools? Chlorine gas can be a problem if a cloud of it rolls over your neighborhood. And what about water treatment plants? Lots of chemicals there. And how about hospitals? There you're looking at a huge range of substances, from infectious to corrosive to radiological.

And last but not least, *your house*. Think about all the chemicals we keep in our garages, sheds, basements, and under our sinks. A fire in any of these locations can create a toxic cloud of completely unknown properties. It's no wonder why fire fighters always wear SCBA to even the smallest fires.

The point of this discussion is to instill the mild paranoia that will keep you alive. Any critical incident can turn into a hazmat scene. Be aware of the potential and be ready with strategies to mitigate the event.

Responding to Scenes

As we've been emphasizing, when you respond to a hazmat scene, chances are good you won't realize you are responding to a hazmat scene. You may receive a report of an MVA, a person down or incoherent, or an explosion or fire.

Although you may have heard of it and scoffed, the "rule of thumb" is an excellent technique for ensuring safe distance from a suspected hazmat scene involving a trailer or tanker. You stop at the point where your thumb, held up at arm's length, can just cover the scene. Obviously, this rule only applies when you've got good line of sight. Use it when you can.

You should have binoculars in your unit and you'd better have a copy of the DOT's *Emergency Response Guidebook*, which we will discuss in Appendix B (see page 175). For now we'll simply say that we believe this book to be as important as your gun and your radio. It can save your life. If you have *any* doubt as to why law enforcement should use this resource, be sure to read the focused discussion in the appendix.

Law enforcement responders frequently fall prey to a machismo that forces them to drive right into unreasonable danger. What kind of cop would stop five hundred yards away from an accident scene when people are obviously hurt and in danger? A smart one. A live one. You can't help anyone if you're incapacitated or dead.

We probably won't change these longstanding attitudes in one book, but we can at least make a start. Our goal, we repeat, is to simply keep you alive and give you the game plan you need to make correct decisions in the first few minutes of a hazmat incident. You have the hard job; you have to make those decisions.

Experience is the Best Teacher

It's frequently hard to get law enforcement officers to take hazmat seriously until they have been directly impacted. In the worst case, a colleague dies immediately. Only slightly less tragic is a slow death that takes days, weeks, or years to occur. Nobody wants to spend one's last years on disability.

When you are exposed even briefly to a hazardous agent, the long-term effects can be both insidious and horrible. Although it would be a good attention-getter, detailing the nature of such effects is beyond the scope of this book. We will instead mention just a few of the immediate logistical implications of exposure.

One of the first things that happens when you even *think* you or one of your team members has been exposed is that you fill out an exposure report. You must, must take this seriously. Many substances create no immediate symptoms. If, down the road, one of your officers begins complaining about chronic headaches or fatigue, you must be able to pinpoint the date of exposure and have an established medical baseline.

Part of the exposure report process is a trip to the hospital. Possibly several trips over the course of a year or more. And of course, many responders simply don't want to go. Excuses abound: "I just got a whiff." "I held my breath." "I showered and washed my uniform as soon as I got off shift." These excuses don't work. Just a few parts per million of some methlab chemicals on your shoes could contaminate your home and endanger your family.

One of the surest ways to impress an officer with the importance of avoiding contact is for him or her to have been subjected to a complete decontamination on a scene. This is an extremely unpleasant experience. Off comes the entire uniform. On comes a little smock. Then you get a lovely and often public trip though a series of children's wading pools getting every inch sprayed and scrubbed.

Most officers need go through this only once to get the message!

Who's in Charge?

In general, law enforcement wants to quickly hand over control of hazmat scenes to the first-responding fire units. This may not be the most appropriate action. Before relinquishing command of a scene, determine the competency level of the fire responder. If they are no more experienced than you, retain command and wait for a specialist to show up. Even then you may remain IC and give the operations position to the hazmat specialist. You may be the better choice to retain overall control of the scene and allow the specialists to focus on containment, evacuation, and/or decontamination.

Some states, such as New Mexico, require that a state police officer assume incident command at hazmat scenes. Frequently it's not so clear. Do a little research to find out what state or local rules may dictate your command response.

So whom can you count on at a hazmat incident? There are several levels of hazmat certification. Each ensures the individual is capable of performing certain duties in any hazmat incident. We'll just quickly review these so you'll know who the players are:

- **Level 1: First Responder.** Also referred to as "Hazmat Awareness," this is the most basic level. Usually a two-day course. First Responders can recognize the presence of hazardous materials, protect themselves, secure the affected area, and call for specialist response.

- **Level 2: Operations.** A more intense 40-hour program. Common for fire and law enforcement supervisors. A person with this certification can act to protect nearby persons, environment, and property from materials release. This person responds defensively to control the release from a safe distance.

- **Level 3: Technician.** These responders can directly control hazardous materials using specialized protective equipment and instruments.

- **Level 4: Specialist.** Very similar to Technicians, except that they have specialized knowledge of response plans, personal protective equipment, and instruments.

- **Level 5: Scene Commander.** This person is responsible for the overall command of a hazmat scene.

Unified Command

We've stressed that fire and law need to work together. Well, there are two federal regulations (OSHA 29 code of federal regulations 1910.120 and EPA code 40 of federal regulations 311) that *require* hazmat responders to initiate ICS and manage through a "unified command" structure.

Over time, many scenes change in nature. These changes require different commanders to take charge of different phases. A typical hazmat scene will start out with just a police response and therefore police command. It may later require triage or removal of injured. In that phase EMS will be in control. Ultimately an event may well end up a fire scene. Once the release is mitigated, the security of the scene and any investigative tasks may fall back on law enforcement officials. This would be especially true in an intentional release situation. Establishing a unified command with representatives from each agency (under one incident commander) ensures a smooth transition through these various stages.

Both the OSHA and EPA regulations have three strict requirements for hazmat response:

- **Use of the "Buddy System."** This is a common fire service tactic in which, for every two responders directly involved with a hazardous material, two additional responders are fully suited and prepared to go in to perform any required rescue. Also called "two in/two out."

- **Use of the Incident Command System.** Covered in detail in Chapter Five (see page 89), ICS provides a flexible set of command staff and operational area functions. Hazmat scenes by their very nature always demand a multidisciplinary approach!

- **Appointment of a Safety Officer.** Although technically part of ICS, the Safety Officer plays a particularly critical role in hazmat incidents. This is the person who does nothing but make sure responders are never put into unreasonable danger.

A tragic example of interdepartmental miscommunication comes from the McKinsey Report on 9/11. A police helicopter hovering over the WTC north tower reported that it could *see* the exposed beams of the building glowing red. It advised the immediate evacuation of the tower. Police and fire maintained separate command posts and that word never got to the fire command. With results we know all too well.

If you find yourself in a situation with two command posts, make sure a police representative with a radio is at the fire command post and vice versa. This is not an optimum solution by any means, but if it's the best you can manage, do it!

Seven Critical Tasks for Hazmat Response

All of the issues raised in Chapter Four on the Seven Critical Tasks apply to hazmat scenes. You can't go far wrong if you focus on your critical tasks.

1. Establish Communications and Control

If possible, clear the current frequency of all routine traffic. Assume and announce your command of the scene. This is critical so that responding hazmat units know who to report to. Provide dispatch with as exact a location for the incident as possible. Report the nature of the incident, wind direction, and relevant topography.

Wind and topography are primary determinants for the extent and path of a release. Wind obviously determines the direction and speed of a plume spread. Topography is obviously important for determining which way a liquid will head. It also affects certain gases. If a gas is heavier than air it will drift down to low-lying areas, such as valley highways and sewers.

Let's make a quick note about wind direction. Some officers may not understand terms like upwind, downwind, windward, or leeward. When giving orders relating to wind direction, be explicit. For example, "Wind is blowing *from* the northwest *into* the southeast. Stay north of the intersection of Main and Second." We define upwind and downwind simply: Upwind means you remain standing up; downwind means you're going down.

2. Identify the Kill Zone

Based on what you know about the nature of the spill and wind and topography, establish a conservative kill zone. Let no one in or out. Somewhere adjacent to the kill zone, establish a decontamination area and an area of safe refuge for dislocated public, if necessary.

3. Establish the Inner Perimeter

Once you establish an inner perimeter, your working area may encompass more civilians. Now you really need to develop a plan for evacuation or shelter-in-place. We will deal with these issues in more detail later in this chapter.

Also take into consideration the safety of the personnel assigned to perimeter duty. If there is substantial danger of inhalation or other contamination, replace them as soon as possible with properly equipped hazmat or fire personnel.

4. Establish the Outer Perimeter

Your primary concern here is that the outer perimeter puts the public at a safe distance from the incident. There have been many examples of releases that forced the evacuation of entire towns. That's a huge perimeter for which you are responsible. Obviously, it is best to man this perimeter with law enforcement personnel, but use non-sworn personnel if necessary. You are probably going to have a large response, so make sure your outer perimeter gives your people room to stage and to maneuver.

Also, continually monitor the outer perimeter to ensure it is a safe distance from the incident. While this perimeter may have been safe when first deployed, factors such as wind conditions and the amount of release can force changes as the incident progresses.

5. Establish the Command Post

As in all incidents, the initial command post will be the first responding supervisor's vehicle. The prime advantage of this is that it is mobile. As we discussed earlier, the advantage of a mobile command post when dealing with a hazmat incident should be fairly obvious. When the wind shifts, you want to be able to close the doors, roll up the windows, and put it in drive. Most hazmat teams have sophisticated mobile command posts.

6. Establish the Staging Area

For the same reasons that you need to establish a large outer perimeter, you need to establish a good-sized staging area. Hazmat units can be double semi trailers and the staging area may also be used as a decontamination area. A decontamination area can consist of anything from one or two inflatable wading pools to sectioned, portable tents capable of processing hundreds of people at a time.

7. Identify and Request Additional Resources

The sooner you recognize that you have a hazmat incident, the sooner you can get the appropriate resources rolling. Question bystanders and victims, if necessary. Use any and all of the techniques we discussed earlier in the chapter to identify the substance. Try to tell the specialists as soon as possible what they're getting into and, as always, direct these resources to the staging area.

Evacuation and Shelter-in-Place

You have two primary methods for dealing with the public impacted by an incident: get them out or protect them in place. Each has advantages and disadvantages. The choice you make depends on your ability to accurately assess the nature of the threat. The essential question is: will the public be safer where they are or will they be safer somewhere else?

There are also numerous legal ramifications associated with each method. Let us be clear that there are few clear-cut laws or precedents associated with public evacuation. These are evolving issues that we as responders have to deal with as they present themselves. All you can do is act professionally and base your decisions on the best intelligence possible.

Evacuation

Evacuation is seldom a first choice. It is obviously disruptive to society and creates numerous logistical problems for police. Evacuation is an option only when you can accomplish it in a *safe* and *orderly* manner. The image of the police unit rolling down Main Street and telling people to simply leave immediately is largely a myth. Such an uncontrolled exodus would be characterized by panic and gridlock. Of course, you can use a bullhorn or PA system if you provide people with the information they need to head calmly in the desired direction.

There are actually two kinds of evacuation:

- **Primary Evacuation** is the initial movement of people out of the kill zone. The first responding supervisor normally carries out this type of evacuation.

- **Secondary Evacuation** is the movement of people from the affected area to a specific location, such as a decontamination site. This type of evacuation is normally based on the analysis and recommendations of a hazmat specialist.

There are some clear guidelines for a controlled evacuation. Police and other first responders from around the country have developed these over many years of trial and error.

- **Always evacuate from a location to a location.** Have a *destination* in mind for evacuees. Don't just drive people from their homes and let them spread across the countryside. If possible, identify a safety zone, such as a high school or other designated shelter, well upwind of the event.

- **Keep a log of those individuals evacuated.** Where's my mother? How can I find my son? Expect these types of questions as soon as word of the evacuation gets out. Make as complete a list as possible including name, contact information, and the location to which an individual was evacuated. Give this list to dispatch, as they will be the first line of defense fielding this sort of call.

- **Clearly mark evacuated locations.** This is critical to ensure officers don't duplicate efforts. You can use colored tape to indicate the status of a particular residence or business. For example, blue for evacuated, red for unable to contact, yellow for in-progress, and so on. This technique leads, unfortunately, to the next tip.

- **Provide security for evacuated locations, if possible.** That colored tape can also serve as a road map for looters. As you mark a mailbox with blue tape and move on, a van may pull into the driveway behind you and clean the place out. Restrict evacuated area access to emergency workers. Check ID of civilians in the area.

- **Remember purses, pills and pets.** Always remind evacuees, if time permits, to bring critical documents, wallets, prescriptions, and pets. Unfortunately, most shelters will not accept animals, so evacuees will likely have to make special arrangements.

Take advantage of available resources, such as your state emergency management agencies. They're waiting for your call! They have personnel and connections that will greatly facilitate your evacuation. They will coordinate with the Red Cross to set up shelters. What's more, they will not try to tell you how to do your job. They are there to help. There is an 800 number available to you. Use it!

The decision to evacuate is usually a tough call, but there is one case in which it's an easy one. In the case of fire or explosion threat, evacuation is mandatory. If there is *any* chance that a person left in the kill zone could provide a point of ignition, they have to go. Imagine a neighborhood sewer filled with gasoline from a tanker spill. Do you really want to leave a bunch of locals smoking in a corner tavern?

Evacuation PR Techniques

We are unaware of any laws that empower law enforcement to evacuate the public from their homes or businesses. All power along these lines lies with elected officials and fire chiefs. That means—in the absence of a state of emergency—we frequently have to be creative. This may require some "dazzling footwork." We heard of one enterprising sergeant in Florida who came up with a unique approach. When dealing with residents who wouldn't leave in the face of Hurricane Andrew, he went back to the office and made up "Next of Kin" notification forms and required holdouts to fill them in. That got their attention.

Another useful technique is to wear a gas mask as you knock on the door. Take it off just long enough to give residents evacuation directions. Trust us, they'll leave!

Shelter-in-Place

The decision to shelter-in-place is usually made by a hazmat specialist based on an assessment of the type of release. Three criteria determine the value of sheltering-in-place:

- **Is it safer?** If the public will be safer in their homes than out on the road or in an evacuation center, leave them there.

- **Can structures be sealed?** Newer building construction is quite tight and, in the event of a chemical or biological release, occupants might be better off staying inside, turning off HVAC systems, and taping off doors and windows (if possible).

- **Does sheltering pose a danger to others?** As we pointed out earlier, if the release involves the threat of fire or explosion, shelter-in-place is not an option.

There is serious discussion underway throughout our discipline about the use of force in evacuation and shelter-in-place scenarios. There is no clear consensus. Many informal class discussions have addressed the issue, specifically in the context of bioterrorism.

Put yourself in this position: You are forced to lock down a large office building because of a confirmed smallpox exposure in the mailroom. Nobody goes in, nobody goes out. Suddenly the president of the company shows up at the front door and insists he be allowed to leave the building. You can't go near him, so physical restraint isn't an option. You definitely can't shoot him. What do you do?

The best solution we can suggest is that you attempt to reason with him. Make it clear that he poses a threat to his family, friends, and community. Also, try to educate him about the course of the disease to which he is suspected of having been exposed. This highlights the need to have a specialist (hazmat or medical) on hand to help you make decisions. Does his leaving pose an immediate threat of death or serious injury to others? If so, you may need to use appropriate force to keep him inside, such as less-than-lethal weapons.

This is just one example of the type of issues we as responders will be called upon to deal with. We will be exploring many such gray areas in the coming years.

Summary

That's it for our 5¢ tour of a $20 topic. Although brief, this extremely focused approach has real value for first-responding law enforcement supervisors. If you don't need detail, don't clutter your mind with it. Focus on what you need to know. Apply the Seven Critical Tasks. Familiarize yourself with the *Emergency Response Guidebook*. Let the specialists do what they do. Work well with others.

Review Questions

1. How would your response differ for an accidental versus an intentional release?

2. Can you name the nine hazardous materials classes?

3. Could you apply the Seven Critical Tasks to a hazmat scene?

4. Can you recall the criteria for evacuation vs. shelter-in-place?

5. Can you describe how law enforcement works with other agencies on hazmat scenes?

Seven

Critical Incident Stress

Objectives

After completing this chapter, you should be able to:

- *Define critical incident stress*

- *Recognize acute and delayed stress symptoms in responders*

- *Identify stress-mitigating techniques for use before, during, and after an incident*

The preceding chapters have covered just about every element of critical incident response…except the one that takes the highest toll on our profession. We have asserted that all incidents share common characteristics. Here is the common result: critical incident stress.

There is no way of knowing the total number of losses law enforcement has suffered due to stress. Cops are adept at masking their emotions. What is known for sure that is every responder to a critical incident experiences stress. All handle it in their own unique ways. Some by processing, others by suppressing.

As with other topics addressed in this book, critical incident stress is a subject worthy of semesters of college-level work. This discussion will be brief because we restrict our focus to stress as it directly relates to the law enforcement supervisor. We'll look at types of stress, how to identify it in your responders, and some guidelines for addressing it. Throughout this book, the underlying theme has been saving officers' lives. Properly identifying and addressing stress can be as critical to an officer's survival as taking proper cover at a scene.

Although attitudes towards stress are changing, there is certainly room for improvement in our profession's awareness and handling of the problem. Just as it is time, we feel, to bring a new response to critical incidents themselves, it is well past time for an enlightened response to critical incident stress.

Sources of Stress

Stress occurs when we are forced to endure an emotionally tragic or physically threatening event. That just about exactly defines the type of incidents discussed in these pages. Gunfire, fatal accidents, hazmat releases…all contribute to stress that can scar the strongest of us.

Some typical events that can create critical incident stress for emergency personnel include:

- The death of someone you tried to save

- A personal threat such as an attack by gunfire

- A fire or explosion that results in death or serious injuries

- Investigating a fatal vehicle accident

- Handling a child abuse incident that results in death or serious injury to the child

The list is virtually endless. It is important to remember that what might be brushed off by one responder could be crippling for another. We're human and we each bring unique experiences, strengths, and limitations to our profession. There is absolutely no shame in experiencing critical incident stress. The only shame is allowing it to go undetected and untreated. It's a shame if you lose a valued friend or colleague to it.

Many factors affect the intensity of critical incident stress. For example, if there is any physical contact with a person you've tried to save, the post-traumatic stress can be greatly magnified. While it is commonly cited as a problem for EMS and fire responders, law enforcement runs the same risk. Attempting a rescue at a traffic accident or dragging a wounded officer out of the line of fire can affect us just as greatly.

There is one stressor particular to law enforcement: the use of deadly force. Next to taking a round ourselves or watching a colleague die, this is perhaps the most stressful event that can happen to an officer. Just about every officer who has used deadly force regrets it. They say they simply had no other choice. They wish it had never happened.

Time and again members of our profession convey their feelings of concern to such officers inappropriately. When an officer uses deadly force, his colleagues may say things such as "great shot" or "you should have shot him again." They're doing the officer a serious disservice. He needs counseling, not locker-room backslapping. Perhaps no personal incident involving the police is more misunderstood by individuals both outside *and within* our profession. Only those directly involved can truly appreciate the impact it has had on their lives.

Stress Types

When one of your responders endures a horrific experience, stress can manifest itself in two ways: acutely and delayed. Each has specific warning signs that you as a supervisor must be sensitive to.

Acute Stress

Acute stress reaction occurs during or shortly after an incident. You can often recognize immediate acute stress in what we call the "thousand-yard stare." You could be standing directly in front of a person and he will not see you.

As Table 7-1 shows, symptoms manifested from acute critical incident stress can be grouped into three broad categories: physical, mental, and emotional. These are things to look for during and immediately after an incident.

Acute Critical Stress Symptoms		
Physical	**Mental (Cognitive)**	**Emotional**
• Nausea • Sweating or tremors • Disorientation • Increased heart rate • Hyperventilation • Crying • Difficulty sleeping	• Impaired thinking process • Inability to concentrate • Confusion • Poor attention span • Forgetfulness • Flashbacks of incident	• Fear of event repetition • Depression and grief • Withdrawal from friends and family • Resentment of others that appear to be handling the incident effectively

Table 7-1: Acute critical stress symptoms.

We'll touch on a few of these in more detail shortly. Watch your responders for these symptoms at your scene debriefing. If you as a supervisor become aware of stress effects in your people, you must take action. Discuss these warning signs with your responders. Be frank and open. And of course, you can't be everywhere at once; ask them to look out for each other.

Crying at a critical incident scene is not unusual. Tears may be of remorse, joy at having accomplished a rescue, or sheer relief at having survived. Unfortunately, there is one particular law enforcement group that is simply not allowed this option: female officers. While women are no more or less likely to experience critical incident stress, they *are* more likely to suppress the symptoms. No female officer wants to reinforce the attitudes of "dinosaurs" who believe policing should be a male-only occupation. There are individuals who would exploit tears as evidence that women simply can't handle the job. Therefore, your female officers are more likely to suppress any and all symptoms of critical incident stress, especially crying. Just one more thing to be aware of.

You *must* discuss flashbacks; they can lead responders to think they are going insane. Flashbacks are a normal cognitive response to stress. But the first time it happens, you can bet they aren't going to volunteer the information. They'll expect to be taken off the streets if they do!

One symptom to which supervisors must pay particular attention to is withdrawal from family and friends. Something that can't be talked about can't be resolved. It really doesn't matter if the discussion takes place with a counselor or informally with the officer support system of friends, relatives, and colleagues. This is where the withdrawal from friends and family can be so debilitating to a law enforcement officer. As a supervisor, you should see a big red flag if an officer has withdrawn from his support system and is not receiving formal counseling.

And lastly, resentment can grow when an officer feels alone in stress response. This usually comes about when other officers involved in an incident mask their feelings and deny any affects. Every responder must feel free to share the personal consequences of an experience. Warn your people that they can damage the effectiveness of an entire team if they suppress rather than process.

Delayed Stress

Delayed or cumulative stress manifests hours, days, or years after an incident. This is when responders frequently begin to exhibit classic characteristics of the "problem" employee. Let's take a look at some of the more common delayed stress symptoms.

As Table 7-2 shows, delayed stress symptoms fall into the same categories as acute responses. We've mentioned that the law enforcement supervisor must keep a close eye on responders immediately following an incident. You should also try to bear in mind long-term effects when dealing with officers exhibiting problem behaviors well after an event. An officer might act normally for a lengthy period of time and then these symptoms could manifest suddenly or gradually.

Delayed Critical Stress Symptoms		
Physical	**Mental (Cognitive)**	**Emotional**
• Frequent and severe headaches • Sleep disorders • Sexual dysfunction • Substance abuse (drugs and/or alcohol) • Loss of energy • Increased use of sick time	• Intrusive mental images of the event • Poor concentration • Nightmares or flashbacks of event	• Marital or family problems • Fear of event repetition • Constant depression • Apathy and cynicism toward work • Defensiveness about problems

Table 7-2: Delayed critical stress symptoms.

Many of these symptoms affect job performance. Apathy, cynicism, or lack of concentration may all be misdiagnosed as disciplinary problems. When you see these behaviors in an otherwise professional, competent colleague or subordinate, alarm bells should go off in your head. Are you dealing with a problem employee or an employee with a problem?

Both 9/11 and the Oklahoma City bombing in 1993 provided graphic examples of normal human response to horrendous events. In the wake of those incidents, indexes of stress-related problems in responders spiked immediately. We won't know the final toll of 9/11 on emergency responders for years. Unfortunately, it's a certainty that additional problems will arise.

But critical incident stress doesn't require an occurrence on those scales. It can result from a hazmat incident on the interstate. It can result from a botched robbery at the corner liquor store.

Strategies

So what can you do to reduce the impact of critical incident stress? While you cannot completely protect your people, there are several strategies you can use to minimize the effects of stress.

- Pre-event planning and training has been shown to have a major positive effect in preparing emergency personnel to more effectively deal with incident stress. If they know what they might face, they can better prepare for it.

- Working together as a team has been shown to provide positive effects for emergency responders. Law enforcement officers tend to work alone, but in critical incidents we are a team. We must be. Train as a team, respond as a team, debrief as a team. Firefighters can return to the firehouse and spend time together after an incident. Officers going back into service in their one-officer units do not have the same opportunity to debrief in a team setting. If you are the team leader (supervisor in charge) during an incident, take steps to make sure your officers spend time afterwards in a group setting.

- Provide training to response personnel on recognizing the symptoms and effects of critical incident stress. Demystify stress. Get it out in the open.

- Making support groups and professional counseling available to emergency workers has shown dramatic results in improving coping skills. Is counseling expensive? Sure it is. But it's money you can't afford not to spend.

A responder suffering from post-incident stress may be hesitant to discuss particulars of the event. The person could be embarrassed or there may be some review of the action underway. For the most part, therefore, counselors simply talk to responders about their own experiences. The most vocal proponents of stress counseling are those who have been there themselves.

Simply hearing what others have experienced can be a major service. More often than not, officers on the receiving end will be experiencing the same emotions and having similar experiences. The main point is for the recipients to realize that they are perfectly normal even when they are experiencing seemingly abnormal symptoms.

One more point needs to be made about peer counseling. It is not privileged communication. Unless the peer counselor can be classified into one of the accepted privileged professions (clergy, doctor, psychiatrist, licensed psychologist, etc.), the conversation is discoverable in a court proceeding. That doesn't mean you shouldn't engage in peer counseling. You just need to be aware of that fact while you are doing it.

During an Incident

As a supervisor, there are steps you can take during a major event to help reduce responder stress. These include:

- Providing effective management and control of the scene

- Making sure personnel take regular breaks

- Ensuring all personnel have adequate and nutritious food and beverages during extended events; avoid caffeine and sugar

- Rotating and relieving workers regularly, making sure relieved workers move away from the scene and rest

Responders to the Oklahoma City bombing scene used many excellent stress-mitigating techniques. These included limiting the time search teams spent in the rubble to a maximum of fifteen minutes at a time. Also, each searcher had access to a "diffuser" on the way out. Defusing is a well-documented technique that helps take the edge off of acute stress at the scene by letting a responder talk to someone immediately. This is supplemental, however; it doesn't replace a full critical incident stress debriefing, which should take place as soon as possible after the incident.

After an Incident

Make it a policy to conduct an after-action review with all personnel involved and encourage them to express feelings and opinions. This doesn't have to be an uncomfortable experience for those unused to sharing emotions. It's simply a venue for some much-needed venting. During this debriefing, remind your people that incident flashbacks are normal and that, among other things, they may initially have difficulty sleeping.

Conduct formal critical incident stress debriefings. Use an experienced and professional counselor and conduct the debriefing as soon as practical after an incident.

And perhaps most importantly, closely monitor the comments, behavior, and attitudes of all personnel involved in the incident. Look for a change from normal pre-incident conduct. A formerly introverted officer that is now the life of the party (or vice versa) should serve as a warning signal that something is awry.

Do everything possible to assist those having problems and arrange for professional counseling, if required. In fact, it is a good idea to put officers who have endured a traumatic experience through counseling whether they want it or not. It certainly won't hurt, and it's likely to uncover problems of which the responder was unaware. Many officers are hesitant to request counseling. This is when you earn your money. The short term, easy route is to ignore the problem or not force the issue. Avoiding the issue does not serve the needs of your officers. Make sure they get the attention they may need.

What is perhaps the worst thing you can do? Create a culture of suppression. Act as if nothing happened. Say things like "I got through it without any therapy. They can too." Awareness starts with you. If you want to shut your people down to dealing with stress, you can probably do it. If you want your people to process the incident so they will be prepared to handle the next one and the one after that, deal with stress openly. Remember our rule of tactical leadership: "everything goes down the lead."

Review Questions

1. Can you recall the types of events that can trigger critical incident stress?

2. Could you recognize symptoms of acute stress in your responders?

3. Could you recognize symptoms of delayed stress in your responders?

4. Can you recall your options for lessening the impact of stress on your responders?

Closing Thoughts

We certainly hope you've gotten some ideas and strategies out of this text. As we pointed out in the introduction, we have a tremendous respect for first responders. All first responders. Every emergency service puts its member's lives on the line every day.

Critical incidents are some of the most intense and stressful events imaginable. If you are able to employ the techniques we have outlined, if the characteristics and shared experiences we've covered help you in any way, we are grateful that you picked up this book.

So what are the common themes we've hit on? Let's summarize quickly:

- Critical incidents share common characteristics. This means you can address most incidents with a common "game plan."

- Our proposed game plan for crisis phase management takes the form of the Seven Critical Tasks. Use these and you won't go far wrong.

- Tactical leadership is essential to an effective, initial critical incident response.

- Know and use the Incident Command System. It's essential.

- We must develop a new respect for and understanding of hazardous materials scenes. Both intentional and accidental releases require many of the same responses.

- Take care of your responders. We all get stressed, but it doesn't have to cripple our ability to live our lives and continue in our jobs.

- Get some training and train realistically. Train like you fight.

Good luck to you.

Vincent F. Faggiano
Thomas T. Gillespie

Appendix A

ICS Task Checklists

All Incident Command System (ICS) positions and functions have specific duties. Unless you implement ICS responses on a regular basis, you're unlikely to remember all of the tasks. Therefore, we have included a summary of those tasks, by position and functional area, in a checklist format.

Because ICS has been around since the 1970s, many agencies and organizations have had a hand in its development. We have adapted these checklists for law enforcement from sources ranging from the National Wildfire Coordinating Group (NWCG) to the Federal Emergency Management Agency (FEMA).

Bear in mind that we certainly don't think that ICS officers can come on to a scene cold and work from a checklist! Get some training. And practice as often as you can.

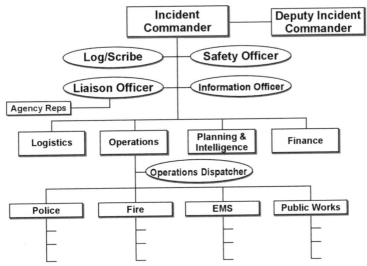

Figure A-1: A fully expanded ICS command structure.

Incident Commander

The Incident Commander (IC) is charged with overall responsibility for all incident activities, including the development and implementation of the Incident Action Plan and approval and releasing of resources. Normally, the first responding supervisor to the scene will assume the role of IC.

❑ If you are the first supervisor to respond, take action to stabilize the scene by initiating the Seven Critical Tasks.

❑ Assess the situation if you are first to assume command, or obtain a briefing from the prior IC.

❑ Select and establish an appropriate command post.

❑ Establish appropriate ICS functions and issue ICS identification badges (which correspond to the specific function assigned).

❑ Determine whether you need a unified command structure with assisting agencies.

❑ Conduct initial briefings of command and section OICs and request that an Incident Action Plan (IAP) with specific objectives be developed for review and approval.

❑ Brief all command post personnel on the IAP.

❑ Continually review and update the IAP with your staff.

❑ Authorize and approve release of information to news media sources and approve plan for returning to normal operations.

Deputy Incident Commander

The Deputy Incident Commander (Deputy IC) is a command staff member appointed to assist the Incident Commander (IC) for a major event. In the absence of the IC the Deputy IC will assume interim command.

❑ Obtain briefing from the IC.

❑ Assist the IC as directed or where appropriate.

❑ Assume interim command when the IC is unavailable or absent from the command post.

❑ Verify execution of IC's directives and compliance with the Incident Action Plan (IAP).

❑ Serve as "Systems Manager:" Make sure that all command post personnel function in their specific roles and that information flows smoothly throughout the command post.

❑ Request that participating agencies provide liaison personnel or agency representatives to the command post when appropriate (this may be delegated to the Liaison Officer).

❑ Review situation or status reports, journals, and other data for accuracy and completeness.

❑ Make sure that all unit logs are submitted to the IC in a timely manner.

Safety Officer

The Safety Officer (SO) is a command staff member responsible for monitoring and assessing hazardous and unsafe situations and developing measures for ensuring personnel safety. The SO will correct unsafe acts or conditions through regular lines of authority, although he or she may exercise emergency authority to stop or prevent unsafe acts when immediate action is required.

❑ Obtain briefing from the Incident Commander (IC).

❑ Assist in the formulation of the Incident Action Plan (IAP).

❑ Monitor operational activities and assess potentially dangerous or unsafe conditions.

❑ Exercise emergency authority to immediately stop or prevent unsafe acts or conditions when appropriate.

❑ Monitor stress levels of involved personnel.

❑ Maintain a log of all activities.

Information Officer

The Information Officer (IO) is a member of the command staff responsible for the formulation and release of information regarding the incident to the news media and other appropriate agencies and personnel as directed by the Incident Commander (IC).

- ❏ Obtain briefing from the IC.
- ❏ Establish a single and separate incident information briefing center, if possible.
- ❏ Obtain or generate all media releases pertaining to the incident.
- ❏ Summarize media coverage in brief reports for specific command post personnel.
- ❏ Obtain approval from the IC for the release of information to the news media. Post all news releases in command post for review.
- ❏ Provide press briefings and news releases as appropriate.
- ❏ Arrange for meetings between news media and incident personnel upon direction of the IC.
- ❏ Provide escort services to the media and other officials as necessary.
- ❏ Maintain a log of all activities.

Incident Log/Scribe

The Scribe is a member of the command staff responsible for maintaining a written log (command post journal) of all incident events and keeping appropriate command post personnel updated on significant developments. The Scribe is also responsible for maintaining an updated map of the incident location or area.

❑ Obtain briefing from Incident Commander (IC).

❑ Maintain an incident log, which will include times, activities, and actions taken.

❑ Periodically distribute a situation report to command post personnel.

❑ Gather incident-related information from other command post personnel for entry into the log.

❑ Forward pertinent information to the Information Officer (IO).

❑ Maintain custody of all documents prepared for briefing the IC; make sure that the date, time, and all persons present for the briefings are properly recorded.

❑ Maintain and display an updated map of the incident location depicting:

- Affected area
- Inner and outer perimeter locations
- Scene command post location
- Staging area location
- Areas requiring evacuation or already evacuated
- Location of assisting agency personnel or specialists

❑ Assist the Planning and Intelligence section to develop a plan for returning to normal operations.

Liaison Officer

The Liaison Officer is a member of the command staff responsible for initiating mutual aid agreements and serves as the point of contact for assisting and cooperating agencies. This could include agency representatives and other jurisdictions with which mutual aid agreements are initiated (fire service, emergency medical services, public works, etc.).

❑ Obtain briefing from the Incident Commander (IC).

❑ Identify Agency Representatives from each responding agency. Identify communications link and location of all personnel assigned to assist with the incident.

❑ Provide an ongoing point of contact for representatives of agencies offering mutual aid.

❑ Handle requests from command post personnel for interorganizational contacts.

❑ Monitor incident operations to identify current or potential interorganizational conflicts or problems.

❑ Provide information to appropriate governmental agencies.

❑ Maintain liaison with the command centers of other agencies involved in the incident.

❑ Maintain an activity log.

Agency Representatives

Agency Representatives are members of the command staff that report to the Liaison Officer or, in the absence of a Liaison Officer, directly to the Incident Commander (IC). Each representative assigned to the command post from another agency is vested with full authority to make decisions on all matters affecting the activities of the agency represented. Only one representative from each agency involved should be assigned to the command post.

❑ Receive briefing from the Liaison Officer or the IC.

❑ Assist with the development or implementation of the Incident Action Plan (IAP), as appropriate.

❑ Provide input on the availability of agency resources and provide technical expertise when appropriate.

❑ Assist and cooperate with all command post personnel in matters regarding agency involvement.

❑ Monitor the wellbeing and safety of agency personnel assigned.

❑ Advise the Liaison Officer of special agency requirements.

❑ Report to agency leaders periodically on incident status.

❑ Participate and assist in demobilization planning. Make sure that all personnel and equipment are accounted for and that all reports are completed before leaving the command post.

Operations Section

The Operations section is responsible for managing the operational units directly related to incident stabilization and resolution. This section is also responsible for assisting in the development of the Incident Action Plan (IAP); specifically in formulating the tactical objectives and operational strategies (the operational component of the IAP).

❑ Assist in developing the operational component of the IAP.

❑ Continually assess the tactical situation.

❑ Execute the operational component of the IAP, with approval of the Incident Commander (IC).

❑ Direct and control the tactical deployment of field elements assigned through the Operations section, which includes Mission Unit Leaders.

❑ Assist the Logistics section in providing all resources (equipment, supplies, and personnel) to field operations for incident resolution.

❑ Make sure appropriate reports are completed for Operations section activities.

❑ Assist with demobilization planning for returning to normal operations.

Operations Officer in Charge

The Operations section Officer in Charge (Operations OIC) is responsible for managing operational units related to incident stabilization and resolution. The Operations OIC is responsible for assisting in the development of the Incident Action Plan (IAP); specifically in formulating tactical objectives and operational strategies. Supervises and directs tactical operations and releases resources as required. Makes expedient changes to the IAP based on field developments and with concurrence of the Incident Commander (IC).

❑ Obtain briefing from the IC.

❑ Supervise and direct the activities of all assigned Operations section personnel.

❑ Coordinate Operations section activities with other field command post units.

❑ Prepare and recommend operational plan changes and revisions to the IC based on field developments.

❑ Issue operational orders to implement the directives of the Operations OIC and IC.

❑ Advise the IC on the readiness of tactical teams for deployment.

❑ Select or recommend staging areas locations, perimeter assignments, evacuation strategies and resource requirements/availability to the field commander.

❑ Provide frequent incident status briefings.

❑ Make sure personnel prepare after-action reports.

❑ Maintain an activity log.

Mission Unit Leaders

Mission Unit Leaders (such as SWAT, Canine Unit, Mounted Unit, and Hazardous Materials Response Unit) report to the Operations Officer in Charge (Operations OIC). They are responsible for conducting specific tactical objectives as assigned by the Operations OIC and formulated under the Incident Action Plan (IAP). Responsible for operational deployment and supervision of assigned personnel only within the scope of their mission.

❑ Obtain briefing and mission assignments from Operations OIC.

❑ Review assignments with team and assign tasks.

❑ Direct, supervise, and monitor mission execution.

❑ Coordinate activities with other field elements and mission unit leaders as required.

❑ Maintain an activity log.

Operations Dispatcher

The Operations Dispatcher reports to the Operations Officer in Charge (Operations OIC) and serves as communications coordinator for radio and telephone traffic at the command post.

❑ Coordinate radio and telephone traffic for Operations section.

❑ Direct field units by radio or telephone as authorized by the Operations OIC.

❑ Coordinate communications activities with other operational agencies involved.

❑ Maintain a dispatch log.

Planning and Intelligence Section

The Planning and Intelligence section is responsible for collecting, evaluating, and disseminating information to measure the size, scope, and seriousness of the incident. It also assists with the development, implementation, and updating of the Incident Action Plan (IAP).

It is also responsible for identifying technical specialists to assist in planning incident resolution strategies. Examples of specialists would be psychologists, environmental scientists, structural engineers, industrial chemists, and so on.

❑ Deploy personnel to gather and assess intelligence information.

❑ Provide intelligence information relating to specific hazardous locations and individuals.

❑ Obtain photographs, audio, and video of the incident where appropriate and assist command post personnel in developing operational response plan.

❑ Monitor all television/radio broadcasts related to the incident.

❑ Assess factors affecting escalation or de-escalation of the incident though field observations, such as identifying high-risk locations, identifying persons inciting violence, estimating damage/injury/casualty situation, and monitoring weather and environmental conditions.

❑ Prepare a plan for returning to normal operations, conduct personnel danger assessment in affected area, and coordinate the reassignment of all incident personnel.

❑ Prepare a plan for repopulation of evacuated areas, where appropriate.

Planning and Intelligence Officer in Charge

The Planning and Intelligence Officer in Charge (Planning OIC) is responsible for collecting, evaluating and disseminating information to measure the size, scope, and seriousness of the incident. This individual also assists with the development, implementation, and updating of the Incident Action Plan (IAP) and identifies technical specialists to assist in planning incident resolution strategies.

❑ Obtain briefing from the Incident Commander (IC).

❑ Provide briefing on incident size and scope to all Planning and Intelligence personnel.

❑ Deploy and supervise personnel as needed to gather and assess intelligence information.

❑ Maintain an intelligence file on specific hazardous locations and individuals.

❑ Direct that all television and radio coverage be monitored.

❑ Prepare estimates of incident escalation and de-escalation at request of IC.

❑ Report to the Safety Officer (SO) or take immediate action for any condition observed which may cause danger or is a safety hazard to personnel.

❑ Prepare a plan for returning to normal operations.

❑ Maintain an activity log.

Logistics Section

The Logistics section is responsible for requesting and/or providing facilities, services, and all resources required for the safe and successful resolution of the incident.

❑ Work with the Operations and the Planning and Intelligence sections to determine the size, scope, and seriousness of the incident and immediate or anticipated resources required for incident resolution.

❑ Request, maintain, and control selected equipment, supplies, facilities, and other services required by the Operations section.

❑ Provide security for the command post, staging area, and other sensitive areas.

❑ Arrange for and provide meals and refreshments for all incident personnel in coordination with other section officers.

❑ Maintain a personnel and vehicle status board to assist Operations Officer in Charge (Operations OIC). Monitor deployment and depletion of personnel and vehicles and advise Operations OIC.

Logistics Officer in Charge

The Logistics Officer in Charge (Logistics OIC) is responsible for providing facilities, services, personnel, and other resources required to assist in the safe and successful resolution of the incident. Participates in the development and implementation of the Incident Action Plan (IAP) and activates appropriate elements of the Logistics section as necessary.

❏ Obtain briefing from the Incident Commander (IC).

❏ Plan and coordinate the activities of the Logistics section and supervise assignment of personnel.

❏ Evaluate with the Operations and the Planning and Intelligence sections the current size, scope, and seriousness of the incident and plan necessary logistical support for field operations.

❏ Coordinate and process requests for additional resources.

❏ Maintain a visible chart of resources requested and advise Operations section of arrival of resources for deployment. The logistical chart should display information as follows:

- Resources requested (available/unavailable)
- Time requested
- Estimated time of arrival
- Location where resource is staged and available
- Descriptive data regarding resource, such as size, numbers, capabilities, and ratings

❏ Maintain an activity log.

Staging Area Supervisor

The Staging Area Supervisor reports to the Logistics Officer in Charge (Logistics OIC). Responsible for establishing and maintaining a location at which personnel and equipment can be staged to provide support and resources to the field commander.

❑ Obtain briefing from the Logistics OIC.

❑ Assist in selecting a location that can be properly secured and is appropriate for staging vehicles and personnel.

❑ Establish a staging area layout and post signs to make sure area can be easily identified.

❑ Determine support needs for equipment, feeding, sanitation, and security.

❑ Maintain a status log and report resource status changes or shortages as required.

❑ Supervise the safeguarding and security of all personnel and equipment.

❑ Demobilize the staging area in accordance with the plan developed for return to normal operations.

❑ Maintain an activity log.

Communications Supervisor

Under the direction of the Logistics Officer in Charge (Logistics OIC), the Communications Supervisor is responsible for providing technical support and developing a plan for the effective use of incident communications equipment, testing and repair of equipment, and supervision of the Communications Center (if established).

❑ Obtain briefing from the Logistics OIC.

❑ Prepare and implement an incident radio communications plan.

❑ Make sure communications center and equipment are operational.

❑ Set up telephone and public address system (if required).

❑ Determine adequacy and geographical limitations of communication systems in operation.

❑ Evaluate equipment capabilities and anticipate problems with equipment during incident.

❑ Inventory equipment availability.

❑ Maintain inventory of all communications equipment.

❑ Maintain an activity log.

Security Unit Supervisor

Under the direction of the Logistics Officer in Charge (Logistics OIC), the Security Unit Supervisor coordinates all activities of the security unit and supervises assigned personnel.

❑ Prepare and submit for approval a security plan for the command post, staging area, and other facilities as needed.

❑ Provide personnel for securing the command post and other areas as directed.

❑ Provide necessary security for staging area to safeguard equipment and personnel.

❑ Provide security escorts to accompany dignitaries to secure areas.

❑ Make sure security posts are manned.

❑ Issue passes to authorized personnel to tour secured areas.

❑ Deny entrance to unauthorized personnel.

❑ Notify the Logistics OIC of individuals requesting to visit command post or other secured areas.

❑ Maintain an activity log.

Personnel Group Supervisor

The Personnel Group Supervisor reports to the Logistics Officer in Charge (Logistics OIC). Evaluates personnel requirements, maintains a master listing of personnel assignments, and performs time-keeping functions.

❑ Obtain briefing from Logistics OIC.

❑ Coordinate personnel to meet the anticipated needs of the Operations section.

❑ Maintain a reserve of personnel to meet the anticipated needs of the Operations section.

❑ Maintain time keeping and assignment location records for all personnel, including mutual aid, volunteers, etc.

❑ Maintain an overtime card file, an assignment file, and a schedule of personnel reassignments or releases.

❑ Brief relief personnel on incident status.

❑ Maintain personnel resources status board and account for all personnel upon initiation of the termination phase.

Finance Section

The Finance Section reports to the Incident Commander (IC) and is responsible for all financial and cost analysis aspects of the incident. Subordinate finance functions may include the Time Unit, Procurement Unit, Compensation Claims Unit, and Cost Unit.

❑ Obtain briefing from the IC.

❑ Activate necessary elements to support Finance section activities.

❑ Provide input in planning sessions on financial and cost analysis matters.

❑ Assist the Logistics section with procurement of equipment, supplies, and other needed resources.

❑ Make sure all personnel time records are maintained and transmitted to agencies assisting with the incident.

❑ Participate in demobilization and termination planning sessions.

❑ Prepare incident-related cost analysis as requested by the Incident Commander.

❑ Respond to and evaluate incident-related compensation claim requests.

❑ Maintain an activity log.

Appendix B

Using the DOT Emergency
Response Guidebook

You've probably seen the little orange book at some time or another. Our goal is to convince you that, beyond being a handy reference tool, the Department of Transportation *Emergency Response Guidebook* (ERG) is a critical part of your practical equipment. Right up there with your gun and your radio.

The ERG coverage in your hazmat class might have been one of those segments that caused your eyes to glaze over. When we've taught classes to hazardous materials IC's and other experts from the fire service, these professionals have asked us why we are able to get law enforcement responders to listen to us. We believe it's *because* we're not experts. We focus on need-to-know information for critical decision making.

And one of the most need-to-know elements for hazmat is the ERG! The ERG is simply one of the best tools you can have available that will help you make those correct decisions. But first you've got to make it available to all of your responders, and then they have to know how to use it.

The federal government publishes the ERG approximately every three years. The books are available to your department for free. You can probably get as many copies as you need through your local emergency management coordinator. There should be one in the glove box of every emergency unit right next to that pair of binoculars. (Remember the rule of thumb? If you can't cover the scene with your thumb, you're *too close!*)

We'll go through the book quickly from front to back and briefly discuss the purpose of each conveniently color-coded section. A quick aside: The term "dangerous goods," which you see on the cover, is simply the Canadian equivalent of "hazardous materials." For the latest information about the ERG, or to obtain a searchable electronic version, go to http://hazmat.dot.gov/gydebook.htm.

Briefly, the ERG sections are:

- **White.** How to use the guide and substance identification tips.

- **Yellow.** Substances listed by universal 4-digit identification numbers.

- **Blue.** Substances listed alphabetically.

- **Orange.** Hazards and response strategies.

- **Green.** Initial isolation distances.

You might want to have a copy of the ERG handy as we discuss each section. That's the best way to see what we're talking about.

White Pages

Among other things, the white pages tell you how to use the book. They also include samples of the placards you might see on some loads. You should at least be able to recognize the colors and numbers of these placards. There is also a cheat sheet of the nine hazardous materials classes. The other handy bit of information here are silhouettes of common trailer and tanker types. This is critical to knowing whether a load is under pressure, liquid, or solid.

The top of page one gives you three things to remember:

- Resist rushing in!

- Approach incident from upwind.

- Stay clear of all spills, vapors, fumes, and smoke.

Yellow Pages

The yellow pages give you a numeric listing of chemicals by their 4-digit identification numbers. This is where you look if you have a placard with a number (1013, 2811, etc.). There are 75 pages of chemicals here. You might think that this represents all of the chemicals produced in North America, but it doesn't. Not by a long shot! The ERG covers only the most commonly transported quarter of that staggering total.

Finding the chemical name is interesting information, but essentially useless. What are you supposed to do about it? Once you find a chemical in this section, you'll notice that it may or may not be highlighted. Based on that you turn to one of two sections for help:

- **No highlighting on entry.** Whether or not the substance is on fire, use the associated guide number to turn to the orange section, which we'll discuss shortly.

- **Highlighted entry.** If the substance is *not* on fire, turn to the green section for isolation distances. If it *is* on fire, turn to the orange section.

Why? Some substances are more dangerous when burning and some are more dangerous when not burning. For example, the entry for "poisonous, flammable gas" (ID 1953) requires an isolation zone of 1 km if it's on fire, but up to 11 km if it's *not* on fire. Good information, don't you think?

Blue Pages

The blue pages give you an alphabetical listing of the thousands of commonly transported substances. Again, there is a 4-digit ID and a guide number associated with each. This section also includes highlighted entries. You use highlighted entries just as you do in the yellow section (depending on whether the substance is burning).

Orange Pages

This is the meat of the book. This is where you find the information you need to make public safety decisions. And because you always make those decisions based on the substance released, you always come to the orange pages through either the yellow or blue section.

This section gives you the data you need to assess risks and provides response guidelines. If you want to take proper action, do what the orange pages tell you to do.

Information for each guide number is always contained on two facing pages. That makes the book easier to handle in the dark with a flashlight.

At the top of each orange page is a guide number associated with every substance listed in the ERG. (Obviously, there are fewer guide numbers than substances. Many substances call for the same response.) Next to the number is a general description of the nature of the substance. For example, it might be listed as a flammable liquid, explosive, mixed load, etc.

Remember the two primary hazmat threats we discussed in Chapter Six? The potential hazards area of each guide number gives you that primary threat: fire/explosion or health. It's in big print right up front because it's the most important information.

One thing you should note is that every one of these guide pages recommends wearing SCBA. Most recommend a chemical suit. And how many of you have these available? Your best defense is distance!

It's not unusual to have no idea at all what you're dealing with. You can still respond appropriately. In this case, turn to the first guide in the orange section, number 111. Use these guidelines to provide a safe response until the exact substance can be identified.

Green Pages

Turn to the green pages to find isolation distances for releases that do not involve fire. Note that this section divides releases into small (200 liters or less) and large (more than 200 liters). For the nonmetric literate, 200 liters is about 50 gallons. When in doubt, assume a large spill.

The other big consideration is time of day. You will notice that isolation zones for spills at night are frequently three or four times as great as those during the day. This is largely due to the difference in atmospheric conditions. A specialist should, if at all possible, decide on the actual size of the isolation zone and whether to evacuate or shelter-in-place.

Glossary

BLEVE: Boiling Liquid Expanding Vapor Explosion. A serious threat from tankers involved in fire.

Buddy System: A common hazardous materials response tactic in which, for every two responders directly involved with a hazardous material, two additional responders are fully suited and prepared to go in to perform any required rescue.

CISD: Critical Incident Stress Debriefing. A service available to emergency responders. Frequently accomplished by teams of first responders with extensive critical incident experience.

Command Post: A central decision-making area established by the Incident Commander to house command staff.

Controllable Factors: Those factors at a critical incident that are within the first responding supervisor's control, such as his own abilities. Should be the primary focus during any response.

Crisis Phase: The first development phase of any critical incident. Characterized by panic, confusion, and responder rush to the scene.

Critical Incident: An extraordinary event that places lives and property in danger and requires the commitment and coordination of numerous resources to bring about a successful conclusion.

Evacuation: Removing the public from homes or business threatened by a critical incident to a safe area.

Executive Management Phase: The third phase of a critical incident characterized by the initiation of an Emergency Operations Center. Only major events evolve to this phase.

Finance Section: An ICS area responsible for all cost and financial matters related to an incident.

Hazardous Material: Any product, chemical, or substance that can cause damage or injury to life, property, or the environment when inappropriately released from its container.

Incident Action Plan (IAP): The resolution plan for an incident developed by the Incident Commander in conjunction with other command staff positions.

Incident Command System (ICS): A highly flexible and modular command structure that enables you to quickly put together a "decision-making team" to manage incidents.

Incident Commander (IC): An ICS position that sets objectives and priorities. This person has the overall responsibility at the incident, including development of the incident action plan (IAP), and the approval and release of all resources.

Incident Log: The record of an event and the decisions taken to resolve it. Critical for post-incident reviews.

Incident Scribe: An ICS function that records an event and the decisions taken to resolve it.

Inner Perimeter: The boundary just beyond the kill zone within which responders operate to directly control an incident.

Integrated Communications: A component of ICS that calls for a comprehensive communications plan and the ability for every agency, section, and unit to be able to talk to every other agency, section, and unit.

Kill Zone: The immediate area surrounding an incident—the area of imminent danger to responders and citizens.

Liaison Function: An ICS position that helps initiate mutual aid agreements and serves as the point of contact between the IC and assisting agencies.

Logistics Section: An ICS area responsible for providing all resources (personnel, equipment, facilities, services, etc.) required for incident management.

MSDS: Material Safety Data Sheet. A brief description of the properties and hazards presented by a material.

Operations Section: An ICS area responsible for all tactical operations directed toward incident resolution.

Outer Perimeter: The perimeter that controls the access to a scene by both responders and the public. The area between the inner and outer perimeters is where responders operate.

Planning and Intelligence Section: An ICS area responsible for collecting, evaluating, and disseminating information regarding an incident. Planning staff asks the "what if" questions.

Primary Evacuation: The initial movement of people out of the kill zone. This type of evacuation is normally carried out by the first-responding supervisor.

Public Information Function: An ICS position responsible for formulating and releasing (with IC approval) all information regarding the incident to the media and other personnel.

Realistic Resources: Those resources, either official or unofficial, that are available in your jurisdiction when you need them. May require some creativity to identify and activate.

Resource Manual: A listing of resources from multiple agencies available to a responding supervisor.

Safety Function: An ICS position responsible for assessing the Incident Action Plan, proposed tactics, and operations with nothing in mind but the safety of responders.

Scene Management Phase: The second phase of critical incident development characterized by the initiation of the Incident Command System.

Secondary Evacuation: The movement of people from the affected area to a specific location, such as a decontamination site. This type of evacuation is normally based on the analysis and recommendation of a hazmat specialist.

Shelter-in-Place: An alternative to evacuation in which public threatened by an incident remain in their homes or workplaces.

Span of Control: A common management concept. Depending on the nature of the task, a supervisor can effectively manage only between three and seven subordinates. Usually averaged to five.

Staging Area: A specific location to which additional resources respond and await deployment to the scene.

Termination Phase: The fourth and final development phase of all critical incidents. Characterized by the post-incident review and return to normal operations.

Two In/Two Out: See Buddy System.

Uncontrollable Factors: Those factors at a critical incident that are beyond the first responding supervisor's control, such as the weather.

USDOT Emergency Response Guidebook: An extremely valuable book listing commonly transported substances and appropriate emergency responses.

Weapon of Mass Destruction (WMD): Any chemical, biological, or nuclear agent designed to kill multiple persons. Many common hazardous materials can be easily converted into WMDs.

Index